HOW ARE YOU PRAYING?

HOW ARE YOU PRAYING?

A MANUAL ON THE PRACTICE OF PRAYER

DONALD E. DEMARAY

Wipf & Stock
PUBLISHERS
Eugene, Oregon

Originally published under the title *Alive to God Through Prayer*, copyright © 1965 by Baker Book House

Wipf and Stock Publishers
199 W 8th Ave, Suite 3
Eugene, OR 97401

How Are You Praying?
A Manual on the Practice of Prayer
By Demaray, Donald E.
Copyright©1985 by Demaray, Donald E.
ISBN: 1-59752-808-0
Publication date 7/5/2006
Previously published by Zondervan Publishing House, 1985

*To
Jack Arnold
Wendell Demaray
Melvin Foreman
Harlow Snyder
Harold Sternberg
Partners in Prayer*

PREFACE

2006 printing of *How Are You Praying?*

My computer screen brings requests for prayer—daily. I like that. Friends share their concerns with me and I with them. The computer has created a whole new world of prayer.

Prayer requests also bring challenges. We know more about the trials and hurts of our friends and acquaintances. In fact, we learn so much that we easily become calloused, even numb.

But depend on this: God's Spirit guides us in our praying. He walks with us through the cries for help, then shows us how to intercede.

I pray God will use this fresh printing of "How Are You Praying?" to comfort, strengthen, and guide us in our private and group experiences.

Donald E. Demaray
Summer 2006

CONTENTS

FOREWORD	9
PREFACE	11
1. HOW TO STAY ALIVE TO GOD	15
2. HOW TO PRAY: A SUGGESTED PATTERN	26
3. HOW TO PRAY FOR REVIVAL	44
4. HOW TO ESTABLISH AND MAINTAIN A PRAYER GROUP	60
5. HOW TO UNDERSTAND THE TEACHING OF THE BIBLE ON PRAYER	79
6. HOW TO PRAY FOR DIVINE HEALING	96
7. HOW TO PRAY WITH YOUR FAMILY	113
8. HOW TO FACE THE CHALLENGES OF PRAYER	126
9. HOW TO PRAY FOR THE SPIRIT'S FULLNESS	143
10. ESPECIALLY FOR MINISTERS AND PRAYER GROUP LEADERS	152
INDEX	169

FOREWORD

I was deeply grateful when I learned of this reprint of a book on prayer by Donald E. Demaray, my esteemed friend and colleague during these many years. And I was honored when I was asked to pen these words in the Foreword. I have prayed with the author many times and have frequently heard him speak on prayer. I know that what he writes about prayer is authentic.

Perhaps some are asking, "Why the reprint of another book on prayer?" The rationale is evident and clear. There is renewed interest in prayer in every part of the Christian world. Never have so many people been so interested in both the meaning and practice of prayer. Such intense interest is manifest not only in personal queries that I receive from every quarter, but also in the fact that an increasing number of books on prayer, from both Protestant and Roman Catholic authors, have appeared on the book market.

However, alongside of such growing interest in prayer, there seems to be increased confusion about prayer. People are asking: "Just what is the nature of prayer?" "What should I pray about?" "What good does it really do to pray?" "Why do some people seem to find it so difficult to get an answer to prayer?"

In this extremely pragmatic age, people insist upon raising the question *How?* in relation to just about everything. And so people want to know *how* to pray.

How Are You Praying? is basically a manual on prayer. It presents a reverent approach to the practical aspects of a life of prayerful communion with God. It is an excellent guide for group study and for training courses as well as for individual instruction and inspiration. Each chapter ends with questions to direct personal thought and group discussion.

The book contains a chapter on the teachings of the Bible on prayer. The author also deals with such intensely practical problems in relation to prayer as: "when prayer is work," "when God seems deaf," "when circumstances are against us," and "when prayer training is difficult and long."

The volume is extremely practical in its *how-to* aspects. The author presents a pattern of daily personal prayer. Much attention is given to praying for specific objectives, such as: spiritual awakening, guidance, family problems, the renewal of the church, and healing. Practical instructions are included for the establishment and maintenance of prayer groups.

How Are You Praying? reveals the carefully documented analyses of the scholar, the deeply spiritual insights of the saint, and the clearly communicated practical advice of the counselor. The book is a source of inspiration and guidance to the spiritually minded person, offers a stimulus to increased experimental participation in the varied aspects of prayer, and becomes an incentive to further intensive study in the entire field.

Frank Bateman Stanger
President Emeritus
Asbury Theological Seminary

PREFACE

Spiritual awakening is the first aim of this book. Prayer is the key and cause of awakening. "What prayer could do in the life of the nation and the world has never really been tried. Millions of people neglect it because they think it is just pious talk and we ought to be 'up and doing something.' To what chaos has their 'up and doing' led! Only when men listen to God can they learn what they should be 'up and doing,' and if they would listen in prayer and obey God's bidding, 'earth would be fair and all men glad and wise.' "[1]

This small book is a plea from a concerned heart to people—especially those who are already baptized church members—to engage in the most rewarding and serious business in the world. It is not only a plea or call to pray, it is a manual on how to pray and what to pray for.

We are close to the real revival we long for so deeply. It is a fact of the world of the Spirit that a great wave of consistent fervent prayer would move the hand of God to unleash his power in the world and thus be the cause of the revival coming to full force. All revivals have been preceded by prayer. World revival has never come. Great revivals have come, but not world revival. Indeed, communism has come closer to stimulating worldwide response than Christianity. The Christian church made some of its greatest advances in the first century. Since prayer is power, not only can the same kind of advances that characterized the Acts of the Apostles come in our age, but a far greater spread of our faith can come with radio, television, jet transportation, and

---

[1] W. E. Sangster, *How to Form a Prayer-Cell*, Westminster Pamphlet No. 10 (London: Epworth, 1958), p. 15.

the other modern methods of communication and transportation.

God grant us such a passion for the lost that we will look forward to the prayer times in the day more than to any other single activity. God grant us hearts that beat faster with excitement at the very thought of communion with Him. God grant us a throbbing, pulsating drive so incurably contagious that people around us will catch the fired heart, thus starting a chain reaction that will lead to global awakening.

The second aim of this book is nurture. Samuel Shoemaker talks about the "two hands of the Holy Spirit." "The right hand is the old, organized, institutional, ongoing historic Church. And the left hand is the new, fresh, spontaneous . . . awakening."[2] The right hand of the Spirit must not be neglected for his left. The continuing round of Christian devotional activity constitutes a big chunk of the material out of which nurture becomes a reality. Thus the imperatives of prayer groups and private devotional experiences. These imperatives have been stressed with the prayer that the Christian faith will be more firmly rooted and grounded in believers. In fact, the book has been designed to be used in prayer groups and study circles, as well as in private devotion. The outline form within chapters and the questions at the end of chapters are calculated to serve the purposes of study guidance and group discussion.

The following have given kind permission to publish quotations. *Decision* magazine, © 1964 The Billy Graham Evangelistic Association, Minneapolis, Minnesota, for use of brief portions from Ruth Bell Graham's article, "Mercy Suits Our Case." The Nazarene Publishing House, for permission to use, in slightly altered form, my article which appeared in *Insights Into Holiness. Youth in Action* magazine for permission to reprint my article, "How to Maintain the Spirit-Filled Life" in altered and expanded form. Moody Press, Moody Bible Institute, Chicago, IL 60610, for permission to quote from V. R. Edman, *Crisis Experiences in the Lives of Noted Christians.*

---

[2]Samuel Shoemaker, *Beginning Your Ministry* (New York: Harper and Row, 1963), p. 103.

PREFACE

The American Bible Society for allowing me to reprint their helpful guide, "Where to Look in the Bible." Epworth Press in London, for permission to quote from W. E. Sangster, *How to Form a Prayer-Cell, Teach Us to Pray,* and *Revival, The Need and The Way.* Christian Literature Crusade for the use of lines in Frank Houghton, *Amy Carmichael of Dohnavur.* Hodder and Stoughton for permission to quote from Samuel Chadwick, *The Path of Prayer.*

To my wife, Kathleen, I owe thanks for helpful suggestions and constant encouragement. To Cornelius Zylstra, editor for Baker Book House, I wish to express thanks for faithful assistance in preparing the first edition of this book.

Donald E. Demaray

SECOND EDITION CREDITS

To the many who requested republication of this book written in conversational style, I must say thank you. "Thank you" also to Harold Burgess, a founder of Francis Asbury Press, for working patiently for this new printing. Further and special thanks to Joseph Allison, editor for Francis Asbury Press, who makes labor a delight.

Donald E. Demaray
Fisher Professor of Preaching
Asbury Theological Seminary

1
HOW TO STAY ALIVE TO GOD

The Spirit-filled life is a deep, full, and satisfying relationship with God. In any relationship between friends, certain things come naturally. In the Spirit-filled Christian's relationship with God, daily Bible reading, daily prayer, and regular group prayer experiences are three things the believer will naturally want to do. When these three activities are part of a Christian's regular experiences, the will to believe is strengthened; but when any component is missing, there comes a feeling that God's Spirit has left. Regular prayer and Bible study are the means of keeping the spiritual power level up to par.

I. DAILY BIBLE READING.

Several years ago, while I was teaching at Seattle Pacific College (now University), a student came into my office, slumped down into a chair, and said, "I thought I was filled with the Spirit, but apparently I haven't been. I see none of the fruit of the Spirit in my life."

I said, "What kind of devotional life do you have?"

"Hit and miss."

"Do you eat your meals that way?"

She answered with a half smile, "I used to and I nearly lost my health."

It was not necessary for me to say, "Is it any wonder you have lost your spiritual health?"

The Bible is food for the Spirit. In order to maintain the Christian life, one must have a beefsteak-sized portion of God's Word daily.

Shortly after my own experience of being filled with the Spirit, it seemed that God's Spirit was leaving me. At once I talked to God. I did not want a temporary experience; I knew I must have a permanent relationship with the Holy Spirit.

God spoke to me as clearly as he has ever spoken: "Read the Bible."

My first impulse was to argue with the Spirit of God: "But I do read the Bible—two or three chapters a day."

The Spirit came back: "That is not enough."

About this time I read of a man who reads six Psalms and two chapters of Proverbs the first thing every morning— the six Psalms to learn how to worship God and the Proverbs to learn how to get along with his fellowmen.

As I read that, the Spirit of God spoke once again: "There's your formula."

Since that day I have read, first thing every morning, six Psalms and two chapters of Proverbs. I can say that even on difficult mornings, by the time I have completed the reading of those eight chapters, my spiritual temperature is up where it ought to be, and I am ready by God's grace and power to begin to shoulder my day's work.

Do not misunderstand me. I am not saying you must read six Psalms and two chapters of Proverbs each morning. That is not mine to say. I have only related what God has assigned me. He himself must make the assignment. God will reveal to you the course your own Bible reading habits must take. Experimentation may be God's way of telling you how much Bible you must read daily to stay alive to him.

Here are some suggestions about what to read in the Bible as you begin and continue the great adventure of Spirit-filled living: John 14–16 constitute the great trinity of chapters that foretell in the words of Jesus the coming of the Holy Spirit. One minister has rightly said that all we need for living the God-dominated life can be found in these three chapters.

Another trinity of chapters is 1 Corinthians 12–14. When these chapters were written, Pentecost had already taken place, so Paul was able to outline the gifts of the Spirit. These three chapters are exciting reading!

From the Acts of the Apostles, the textbook on the Holy Spirit, you will learn more about the true church than in any other book of the Bible.

Get God's assignment for daily Bible reading. Ask Him for the discipline to do what He says. Then in *his* power— not *yours* —follow through on your assignment.

II. DAILY PRAYER.

John Wesley prayed one hour every morning and another hour each evening. E. Stanley Jones did the same; perhaps he took the hint from the father of Methodism. Not everyone is called upon to pray that much; if you are, thank God for the gift of much praying, because the rewards are rich.

But let's be realistic. Young Christians normally would find two hours of prayer a chore if not a bore. The late W. E. Sangster, famed Methodist preacher of London, suggested what we might call the "15–10 program"—fifteen minutes in the morning and ten at night. Anyone can do that.

It will take time to learn to pray even that long, but if you remember that prayer time is in a sense the most intimate part of your relationship with God, it will soon become easy. Many will find the "15–10 program" is not enough time to be alone with God.

If Christ is the Lord of your life, it follows that he is the Lord of your time. Conversely, if Christ is not the Lord of your time, how can you honestly say he is Lord of your life?

I have watched a young mother whose life is filled with the daily round of astonishingly busy activity. Children *are* demanding! Yet I have seen her snatch moments for prayer when the house is momentarily empty of children and at other times. Her reasoning is very practical: "If I wait for a stretch of time later in the day I am only kidding myself. There is no stretch of time with little children in the home. Therefore, I will take the five minutes (perhaps only two minutes) I have right now. And then other patches of time in the day I will snatch, too."

But why pray every day? Because the Spirit-filled person can lose his relationship even as one can lose a human friendship—by avoiding his friend. Friendship with God is lost by ignoring him. The subtle problem is just this: Friendship is lost a day at a time, and because it is lost no faster than that, we can slowly but surely be blinded to our loss of God. Therefore, *prayer must be daily.*

Take the problem of on-the-spot temptation—temptation that is totally unexpected. The weapon is on-the-spot prayer. In the moment of temptation, lift up a quiet prayer within yourself: "Oh, God, I need your help right now." This kind of prayer works.

Or take the problem of failure. Suppose one does yield to temptation—says a cross word, laughs at an off-color story, does something to grieve God. This is no reason to throw over one's experience. On the spot, lift up a prayer pleading for forgiveness, then go right on living the Spirit-filled life, asking God for power against failure next time.

Or take the problem of wandering thoughts in prayer. The answer to that is to take your thoughts, wandering though they are, and lift them up into the very fabric of your prayer. Suppose I am praying for Jane and my thoughts run to Bill. I catch myself in this wandering thought. Instead of berating myself for having thought of Bill, I pray for him and *then* pull my thoughts back into line.

A further solution to wandering thoughts is the use of a prayer list. Become specific. The very fact that your prayer needs are listed helps to keep you from wandering. Buy a small notebook in which to keep a list of the needs and the people God lays on your heart.

Also take time to thank God for prayers that are answered. It is not enough to ask. We are obliged to thank as well. The Spirit-filled person knows the blessedness of praising God.

III. PRAYER WITH PEOPLE.

Jesus promised that where two or three are gathered together in his name, he would be with them (Matt. 18:20).

Something happens in group prayers that does not happen in private. In the group each is made aware of the needs of the others. Prayers are made accordingly. If prayer is always private, it can become self-centered.

In finding a prayer partner or two, ask God for likeminded people. One of the signs of a Spirit-filled person is that he talks freely about the things of God. This is the kind of person with whom to pray on a regular basis. In a pagan culture it may be hard to find such a person. Then ask God for a prayer partner. In your own local church you may find one. A new convert is especially alive to God; he will pour fresh enthusiasm into your prayer life.

No revival of religion has come in all of the history of Christianity without group prayer. Thus it is necessary to the life of the church as well as to the lives of individual Christians.

IV. SOME HINTS.

The Christian who has a long-established habit of daily prayer and Bible reading knows that days, weeks, months, and years of communion with God have, altogether, a great deal to do with the effectiveness of petition at times of greatest need. A godly professor had three centers in his study: a desk where he wrote his books and articles, an easy chair where he liked to read, and a prayer desk where he studied his Bible and entered into daily communion with God. The prayer desk was as important as the other two centers. Years ago the professor determined to be regular about prayer and it became as daily and natural as breakfast.

A. Set Your Will.

Of course, even a modest beginning takes determination. *Set your will.* Decide once for all that nothing short of an earthquake will stop you—and not even that, for you can set your prayer time later in the day. But it is easy to discover excuses for not praying; indeed, the excuses come flooding in! And how good the reasons can be. As if doing things other than praying were more important! But we must not allow the good to become the enemy of the best. The development of the life in the Spirit requires strict attention to prayer and devotion. We must give ourselves without reservation if we are to grow in the things of God. W. E. Sangster says, "Growth in the mind of Christ demands iron firmness with ourselves in our fixed periods of prayer."[1] "My vows to thee I must perform, O God . . ." (Ps. 56:12).

"Iron firmness," however, will not work unless the will has actually been set. To *say* "I will" is different than to *mean* "I will." The daily practice of prayer requires determination from the deepest part of your being. Catherine Marshall LeSourd tells the story of her young step-daughter's struggle to wear a retainer, a plastic device to assist in straightening the teeth. Wearing it is no picnic, as anyone who has had one can testify; but using it is imperative and demands faithful daily attention. Repeatedly, however, Linda forgot to put it on, and the whole affair came to a crisis when one day she left it in the restroom of a train, only to remember it after she had gotten off the train. Her mother explained to Linda the necessity of *setting her will* to remember to wear the retainer. Once that was done—really done—Linda began to get help.[2]

B. Setting the Will With God.

There is a divine side to the setting of the will. Catherine prayed earnestly with Linda about her problem. "You can try to wear the retainer by dogged will-power," said Mrs. LeSourd. "But Linda, there's a much better way. If you tell God that you're willing to have him change you, so that you'll like doing what you must do, then he will. It really works."[3] It was only after several bedtime prayers of such earnest asking that Linda was on her way to a solution of the problem.

God himself must help us in the act of willing, especially

---

[1] W. E. Sangster, *The Secret of Radiant Life* (Nashville: Abingdon, 1957), p. 177.
[2] Catherine Marshall, *Beyond Our Selves* (New York: McGraw-Hill, 1961), pp. 60–62.
[3] Ibid., p. 62.

as it relates to a regular prayer discipline. A missionary friend confessed, "I don't have a daily quiet time. I try. I say 'I will,' then I don't." I assured him that the power of God's Spirit could change that. We prayed for God's Spirit to infill him. God answered that prayer, and his subsequent letters from the field indicate he has learned something of what it is to secure his discipline from the Author of Discipline.

C. The Great Aim of Daily Prayer: To Become Like Jesus.

Why all of this emphasis on prayer anyway? Is it really necessary that the Christian commune with God every day? Why not just occasionally?

Without prayer there simply is no progress toward becoming like Christ. The more we pray—if it is truly prayer—the more we become like Jesus. We have heard of, or perhaps known, a husband and wife who took on one another's characteristics; their admiration for each other, coupled with the fact that they spent a good deal of time together, resulted in their similarities. So it is with our relationship to Christ. When we live with him we become increasingly like him.

Ponder that fact! To become like Jesus—this is the great goal of every honest Christian. It is therefore no exaggeration to say that praying is the most important thing you can do in the course of any day. This significant activity will attune you to God, assist you in living successfully with others in the workaday world, provide the inner resource to live in harmony with your family (how many cross words prayer could remove from the family circle!), and keep you at peace with yourself (since prayer releases you from yourself).

D. "Feeling" Is No Guide.

Suppose, however, that even though I know full well the aim and benefits of prayer, I still do not *feel* like engaging in it? Feeling is no guide to the practice of prayer.

If I have an appointment to preach on a given evening in Cincinnati, I cannot let my feelings dictate whether I will go.

HOW ARE YOU PRAYING?

I may have had a hard day, find myself weary, and quite out of the "mood" of boarding a plane and preaching an evening service. But I will go to Cincinnati. I have made the commitment in advance. Courtesy alone dictates that canceling is legitimate only in the event of emergency. I will go to Cincinnati whether I feel like it or not, ask God's restorative blessing for my body and mind, and expect his Spirit to touch lives in my audience.

Praying daily must have about it that same sense of obligation. And to keep the appointment with God is sooner or later to know the immense benefit of the touch of his Spirit.

Most people seasoned in prayer have learned methods of getting themselves in a mood for prayer. Reading or singing a hymn will do it for some. The late Mrs. Mary Slosser, missionary to the Chinese, used to say, "I sing the Doxology and dismiss the devil!" Like Mrs. Slosser, Amy Carmichael knew the power of song to set the mood of prayer. "I believe truly," she said on one occasion, "that Satan cannot endure it [song], and so slips out of the room—more or less!—when there is true song. . . . Prayer rises more easily, more spontaneously, after one has let those wings, words and music, carry one out of oneself into that upper air."[4]

Simply sitting still and quieting one's heart, mind, and body will do it for others—this was one of Japanese evangelist Toyohiko Kagawa's methods. As God told the psalmist, "Be still, and know that I am God . . ." (Ps. 46:10a).

Others have found a meaningful verse of Scripture sufficient to stimulate prayer. George Müller used this technique each day as he prayed for the needs of his orphanage in Bristol, England.

Reading a page from a good devotional guide is apt to get results. Some especially helpful devotional resources of this type are William Barclay's *Everyday Prayers;* E. Stanley

---

[4]Quoted by Frank Houghton, *Amy Carmichael of Dohnavur* (Fort Washington, Pa.: Christian Literature Crusade, n.d.), p. 321.

Jones's *Abundant Living* and *Victorious Living;* and the daily devotional magazine *The Upper Room.*

But being human, you may have days when none of these devices work. Amy Carmichael, sainted missionary to orphans of India, confessed on one occasion that she had failed "rather badly" at praying; yet she learned something: "Last night, after trying to pray, and failing rather badly, I turned to a small book of Isaiah that lay by me, and those words about the gates of Zion caught my eye. 'Thy gates shall be opened continually; they shall not be shut day or night.' Like the lovely words in Revelation about the gates of pearl which are not to be shut at all, I suppose they are figures of the truth. The gates of access into the Father's presence are open, continually. There is no need to push—perhaps 'trying to pray' is sometimes a sort of pushing. This was how it came to me—*If the gates are open there is nothing to do but go in.* It sounds too simple to tell, but it helped me very much."[5]

. . . But one more thing must be said about praying even when one does not feel like it. It is simply this: At those very times, we need prayer most and it may do us the most good. So pray daily whether you feel like it or not. Soon you will make the exciting discovery that there is spiritual energy in prayer and that you simply cannot do without it.

APPENDIX

Where to Look in the Bible*

WHEN:

Desiring inward peace—John 14; Romans 8.
Everything is going well—Psalms 33:12–22, 100; 1 Timothy 6; James 2:1–17.
Satisfied with yourself—Proverbs 11; Luke 16.
Seeking the best investment—Matthew 7.
Starting a new job—Psalm 1; Proverbs 16; Philippians 3:7–21.
You have been placed in a position of responsibility—Joshua 1:1–9; Proverbs 2; 2 Corinthians 8:1–15.
Making a new home—Psalm 127; Proverbs 17; Ephesians 5; Colossians 3; 1 Peter 3:1–17; 1 John 4.

---

[5] Ibid., p. 318.
*Reprinted by permission of the American Bible Society.

HOW ARE YOU PRAYING?

You are out for a good time—Matthew 15:1-20; 2 Corinthians 3; Galatians 5.
Wanting to live successfully with your fellowmen—Romans 12.
Anxious for dear ones—Psalm 121; Luke 17.
Business is poor—Psalms 37, 92; Ecclesiastes 5.
Discouraged—Psalms 23, 42, 43.
Everything seems to be going from bad to worse—2 Timothy 3; Hebrews 13.
Friends seem to go back on you—Matthew 5; 1 Corinthians 13.
Sorrow overtakes you—Psalm 46; Matthew 28.
Tempted to do wrong—Psalms 15, 19, 139; Matthew 4; James 1.
Things look "blue"—Psalms 34, 71; Isaiah 40.
You seem too busy—Ecclesiastes 3:1-15.
You can't go to sleep—Psalms 4, 56, 130.
You have quarreled—Matthew 18; Ephesians 4; James 4.
You are weary—Psalm 95:1-7; Matthew 11.
Worries oppress you—Psalm 46; Matthew 6.

IF YOU:

Are challenged by opposing forces—Ephesians 6; Philippians 4.
Are facing a crisis—Job 28:12-28; Proverbs 8; Isaiah 55.
Are jealous—Psalm 49; James 3.
Are impatient—Psalms 40, 90; Hebrews 12.
Are bereaved—1 Corinthians 15; 1 Thessalonians 4:13-5:28; Revelation 21, 22.
Are bored—2 Kings 5; Job 38; Psalms 103, 104; Ephesians 3.
Bear a grudge—Luke 6; 2 Corinthians 4; Ephesians 4.
Have experienced severe losses—Colossians 1; 1 Peter 1.
Have been disobedient—Isaiah 6; Mark 12; Luke 5.
Need forgiveness—Matthew 23; Luke 15; Philemon.
Are sick or in pain—Psalms 6, 39, 41, 67; Isaiah 26.

WHEN YOU:

Feel your faith is weak—Psalms 126, 146; Hebrews 11.
Think God seems far away—Psalms 25, 125, 138; Luke 10.
Are leaving home—Psalm 119; Proverbs 3, 4.
Are planning your budget—Mark 4; Luke 19.
Are becoming lax and indifferent—Matthew 25; Revelation 3.
Are lonely or fearful—Psalms 27, 91; Luke 8; 1 Peter 4.
Fear death—John 11, 17, 20; 2 Corinthians 5; 1 John 3; Revelation 14.
Have sinned—Psalm 51; Isaiah 53; John 3; 1 John 1.
Want to know the way of prayer—1 Kings 8:12-61; Luke 11, 18.
Want a worshipful mood—Psalms 24, 84, 116; Isaiah 1:10-20; John 4:1-45
Are concerned with God in national life—Deuteronomy 8; Psalms 85, 118, 124; Isaiah 41:8-20; Micah 4, 6:6-16.

TO FIND:

The Ten Commandments—Exodus 20; Deuteronomy 5.

HOW TO STAY ALIVE TO GOD

The Shepherd Psalm—Psalm 23.
The Birth of Jesus—Matthew 1, 2; Luke 2.
The Beatitudes—Matthew 5:1-12.
The Lord's Prayer—Matthew 6:5-15; Luke 11:1-13.
The Sermon on the Mount—Matthew 5-7.
The Great Commandments—Matthew 22:34-40.
The Great Commission—Matthew 28:16-20.
The Parable of the Good Samaritan—Luke 10.
The Parable of the Prodigal Son—Luke 15.
The Parable of the Sower—Matthew 13; Mark 4; Luke 8.
The Last Judgment—Matthew 25.
The Crucifixion, Death, and Resurrection of Jesus—Matthew 26-28; Mark 14-16; Luke 22-24; John 13-21.
The Outpouring of the Holy Spirit—Acts 2.

FOR DISCUSSION

1. Do you believe the infilling of the Spirit can change one's prayer life? Why or why not?
2. Do you believe each of the three ways of staying alive to God is indispensable? Why or why not?
3. What is the source of our discipline for daily prayer and devotion?
4. Why is "feeling" no reliable guide to prayer?
5. What is your solution to wandering thoughts during prayer?
6. What is your view on how much Bible should be read daily? Or is it a matter of "how much" at all?
7. Do you belong to a small prayer group? What are the benefits you realize from this weekly experience?

BIBLIOGRAPHY

Baillie, John. *Christian Devotion*. London: Oxford University Press, 1962.
Barclay, William. *A Book of Everyday Prayers*. New York: Harper, 1959.
Houghton, Frank. *Amy Carmichael of Dohnavur*. Fort Washington, Pa.: Christian Literature Crusade, n.d.
Jones, E. Stanley. *Abundant Living*. New York: Abingdon, 1942.
———. *Victorious Living*. New York: Abingdon, 1936.
Marshall, Catherine. *Beyond Our Selves*. New York: McGraw-Hill, 1961.
Sangster, W. E. *Teach Us to Pray*. London: Epworth, 1951.
———. *The Secret of Radiant Life*. Nashville: Abingdon, 1957.
The Upper Room. A devotional quarterly published in Nashville, Tenn., by The Upper Room.

2

HOW TO PRAY: A SUGGESTED PATTERN

No one knows how to pray as he ought. But this should not stop us from praying, nor from learning more and more about how to pray. The way to learn to pray is to pray. The purpose of this chapter is to offer a suggested approach or pattern for prayer.

I. THE FIRST THOUGHTS OF THE DAY SHOULD BE OF GOD.

Make a habit of thinking about God as soon as you wake up in the morning . . . even before you get out of bed. The psalmist said, ". . . When I awake, I shall be satisfied with beholding thy form" (Ps. 17:15). This is to start the day right. The first thoughts tend to color the whole day, and if the first thoughts are of God, the day will be tinted with light, bright hues instead of dark, dull ones. This habit is one key to mental composure. And isn't composure needed to get the children dressed, fed, and off to school? Or if your children are grown, or you have none, it is still a chore to get the day started with unnecessary grumbling and discoloration. Start your morning in the spirit of Edward Caswall's great hymn:

> When morning gilds the skies,
> My heart awakening cries
> May Jesus Christ be praised:

HOW TO PRAY: A SUGGESTED PATTERN

> Alike at work and prayer
> To Jesus I repair;
> May Jesus Christ be praised.

Some find the Devil trying to sidetrack them into thinking negative thoughts first thing in the morning: unhappy tasks to be done, too many tasks, inability to do them. But notice the second verse of Caswall's hymn:

> Does sadness fill my mind?
> A solace here I find.
> May Jesus Christ be praised:
> Or fades my earthly bliss?
> My comfort still is this,
> May Jesus Christ be praised.

The first thoughts upon waking should be of God.

II. HAVE YOUR MORNING QUIET TIME AS EARLY IN THE DAY AS POSSIBLE.

Not everyone is made to get up early in the morning, but if you are, or can adjust to it, thank God! It gives one a sense of getting a "head start" on the day—especially if the day is begun with God. "It is good to give thanks to the Lord, to sing praises to thy name, O Most High: to declare thy steadfast love in the morning, and thy faithfulness by night . . ." (Ps. 92:1–2). The exhilaration of the early morning hours is in itself rewarding; with God it is doubly so.

> Still, still with thee, when purple morning breaketh
>   When the bird waketh, and the shadows flee;
> Fairer than morning, lovelier than daylight,
>   Dawns the sweet consciousness, I am with thee.
>   —Harriet Beecher Stowe

The very stillness of the morning lends itself to prayer. The children are asleep; the house is quiet; only the sounds of nature are heard.

> Alone with thee, amid the mystic shadows,
>   The solemn hush of nature newly born;
> Alone with thee in breathless adoration,
>   In the calm dew and freshness of the morn.

It is no wonder the psalmist said, "O LORD, in the morning thou dost hear my voice; in the morning I prepare a sacrifice for thee, and watch" (Ps. 5:3). In Psalm 92:2 we are admonished "to declare thy steadfast love in the morning. . . ."

If your day is oriented toward God—if it is begun right—what a difference it makes! If you are not an early riser, at least find a quiet fifteen minutes sometime before breakfast.

III. USE A PRAYER LIST: AN ANSWER TO HIT-AND-MISS PRAYING AND WANDERING THOUGHTS.

A key to effective praying is the habitual use of a prayer list. If carefully made out, in the light of the needs around you and at the promptings of the inner voice of God's Holy Spirit, the prayer list has the immense twin values of (a) holding you to specific concerns and (b) preventing in some measure the plague of wandering thoughts. Non-directed prayer becomes a rambling sort of thing which almost certainly lacks full, ordered meaning. To allow prayer time to degenerate into a mere string of thoughts is wool-gathering, not prayer. Ordinarily, even when the thoughts are pulled back into line and connected once again into prayers, the line of unconnected thoughts returns and one is wandering once more, unless a prayer list is used.

Of course, even with a prayer list you must exercise discipline to prevent wandering thoughts. But at least there is a numbered outline in black and white and the sheer visibility of it jars you back to specific matters and concentration. One of my friends put it this way: "If you are going to pray, you might as well mean business. The best way I know how to 'mean business' is to keep a prayer list."

Your prayer list should be updated and varied with the changing needs of the people in your circle of knowledge. To use the same list week in and week out will turn your quiet time into boredom. Add names and needs as the Spirit directs them to your attention. This means a constantly growing list, and growth brings variety and interest. Do not

HOW TO PRAY: A SUGGESTED PATTERN

fall into the dilemma of thinking you must get through your list every day. Indeed, you might keep a kind of "urgency list" like the following, separate from the general prayer list:

- The pastor's wife desperately ill.
- Johnny Jones on the verge of committing his life to Christ. .
- Betty Sue debating marriage to that non-Christian boy.

Get through the brief urgency list regularly. Let the larger list follow a more flexible course, but without piling up names carelessly.

Leave a place too in your prayer notes for answer to prayer. It is a great morale factor to have this "documented" evidence of answers to prayer. Nothing is more exhilarating or more encouraging than to praise God for answered prayer. Buy a small notebook; on one side put a list of requests, on the other side answers.

IV. THE 15-10 PROGRAM.

A certain minister of the gospel prays an hour in the morning and an hour in the evening—he never misses this prayer appointment, even if he is in an air terminal or on a bus. He has learned to shut out the noises and absorb himself in God. Perhaps this daily pattern was suggested by John Wesley who early in his youth resolved to spend an hour each morning and evening in prayer, a promise he never failed to keep. Busyness—and John Wesley *was* busy!—never cut short his private time with God. Wesley's remarkable energy and creative ideas were surely given because of prayer.

Begin your own prayer program by setting aside fifteen minutes in the morning and ten at night. This was Dr. Sangster's suggestion to beginners.[1] Lengthen the time as God leads, but begin modestly. It is self-defeating to begin on, say, Wesley's two-hour a day program, only to find yourself failing. Sangster's fifteen-ten minute program is

---

[1] W. E. Sangster, *Teach Us to Pray* (London: Epworth, 1951), p. 21.

realistic—anyone serious about learning to pray can do that much.

V. SUGGESTED PROCEDURES.

A. Begin With the Adoration (Praise) of God.

The praise of God should have first place in your prayers. Prayer about yourself, whether petition or thanksgiving, should come *after* your orientation to God has been fixed. God is to be praised for himself, for what he is and who he is. This praise he wants just as human beings do, for one of the characteristics of personality is the desire to be loved and appreciated. (In this respect, as in others, we are created in the image of God.)

The Book of Psalms is an excellent source book in the praise of God. It is in fact a book of praises, the hymnbook of the Old Testament temple. "I will bless the LORD at all times: his praise shall continually be in my mouth. My soul makes its boast in the LORD; let the afflicted hear and be glad. O magnify the LORD with me, and let us exalt his name together!" (Ps. 34:1–3). The Psalter reaches into every aspect of human experience—death and life, sickness and health, failure and success—and thus has the enormous benefit of meeting our own deep needs while uttering praise to God. Therein is a law of the spiritual life: To praise God is to be blessed (helped) by God. Some Psalms to concentrate on during the stage of praise are 1, 19, 23, 46, 84, 91, 100, 118, and 150. But read the whole book over and again regularly. It will build into your life a vital and solid faith.

A modern hymnbook is also an excellent guide to the adoration of God. A hymn is quite literally a "song of praise or adoration." The following aspects of Christian life and faith probably are addressed in your hymnbook:

> The Worship of God
> The Trinity
> God the Father
> God the Son
> God the Holy Spirit
> The Bible

HOW TO PRAY: A SUGGESTED PATTERN

    The New Birth
    The Spirit-Filled Life
    The Christian Family
    The Sacraments

The private singing or saying of the Doxology is an excellent way to engage in the praise of God:

> Praise God, from whom all blessings flow;
> Praise Him all creatures here below;
> Praise Him above, ye heav'nly host;
> Praise Father, Son and Holy Ghost.
> —Thomas Ken

George Herbert's hymn of 1633 is another classic example of praise:

> Let all the world in ev'ry corner sing,
>   My God and King!
> The heav'ns are not too high,
> His praise may thither fly:
> The earth is not too low,
> His praises there may grow,
> Let all the world in ev'ry corner sing,
>   My God and King!
>
> Let all the world in ev'ry corner sing,
>   My God and King!
> The church with psalms must shout,
> No door can keep them out;
> But, above all, the heart
> Must bear the longest part
> Let all the world in ev'ry corner sing,
>   My God and King!

The hymnody of the church on the Holy Spirit is rich indeed, especially George Croly's "Spirit of God, Descend Upon My Heart" and Edwin Hatch's "Breathe on Me, Breath of God." The hymns in praise of Christ are equally vigorous in their spiritual thrust, and none is better than Charles Wesley's on Christ's suffering and death:

> O Love divine, what hast thou done!
> Th' incarnate God hath died for me!
> The Father's co-eternal Son
> Bore all my sins upon the tree!

HOW ARE YOU PRAYING?

> The Son of God for me hath died:
> My Lord, my Love, is crucified.

Go then to your own hymnbook—if you don't own a good one, by all means get one right away—and use it daily. Someone has said, with more insight than humor, "A hymn a day keeps the Devil away."

Frequently we need to utter, quietly and in privacy, the simple declaration, "Praise God." In the moment of depression, illness, or temptation, audibly reminding ourselves to "praise God" will tend to bring the release that restores courage and normalcy.

B. Offer Thanks to God.

Just as God delights in being loved and praised, so he wishes to hear the word of thanks. There will be special and specific answers to prayer for which to offer your thanks. But do not overlook the everyday blessings, without which we would be unhappy, if not handicapped:

- Health
- Home
- Children (or Grandchildren)
- Books
- Friends
- Music
- Nature

1. *Health.* Do you take time to say a simple "thank you" to God for physical well-being? Even if you suffer from some minor or major ailment, you have health enough to carry on with your work. If you have not that much health, you are still alive. If death is knocking at the door, your health is soon to be perfect with Jesus.

2. *Home.* What a warm divine gift is your Christian home! Do you thank God for it? Think of the domestic influence of Christ, his felt presence, sharing his Word at family worship and at other times. Express your gratitude to God for a Christian wife or husband, for children growing up in the Sunday school, for your church, for its youth programs and other family-oriented ministries, and so on.

HOW TO PRAY: A SUGGESTED PATTERN

Or meditate thankfully upon the material blessings that help to make your house a home: the warm greeting of an attractive wife upon coming home from work in the evening, the laughter and liveliness of children, the crackle of a fire and the charm of the fireplace, the aroma of dinner in preparation. All these make up that magic place called "home." Thank God for this little foretaste of heaven.

3. *Children (or Grandchildren).* To be sure, they are frustrating at times, but children are priceless gifts of God. Their charm and creativity keep us alive and make us the more human. The fun of making or buying clothes for them, of dressing and fussing over them, lend variety to life. Parents find meaning and purpose for their lives because they are responsible, under God, for their children's well-being and education. Thank God for your children. Pray every day for the salvation of your children. How sad to think of losing a single one to sin!

4. *Books.* They "stretch the mind a bit," said Principal John Baillie. Books enlarge our knowledge, raise our horizons, and strengthen life's purposes. Books are our friends.

If you feel the need of a spiritual "refresher course," let a book be your teacher. If your need is devotional, read from the great masters of prayer such as E. M. Bounds, E. Stanley Jones, and W. E. Sangster. Other spiritual needs may be met by reading poetry, fiction, history, and so on. In fact, part of the Bible's genius lies in its rich variety of literary form.

Or think of the miracle of any book. This marvelous tool—with a cover, pages, readable print—has not always been at the disposal of mankind. Centuries passed with no book; stones, tablets, and scrolls were used for communication. Then someone conceived of making the book. What an immense benefit! Printing as we know it in the Western world is of comparatively recent origin (fifteenth century); with its advent, the manifold delights of reading were made available to the masses.[2] The book! Think of it and be thankful.

5. *Friends.* What would life be without them? They

---

[2] It is sobering to think of the painstaking and pioneering work of printers like Gutenberg and Caxton; one cannot help but lift up a prayer of gratitude for them and the printing craftsmen who have followed them.

provide escape from loneliness, add zest to life, make fun and fellowship possible, and provide assistance when in trouble. Christian friends contribute to the nourishing of life in the Spirit; indeed, they are the true church. A compassionate friend can sift out your eccentricities and be content with you just as you are. A friend who is morally, spiritually, and intellectually strong makes you a better person—"Iron sharpens iron, and one man sharpens another" (Prov. 27:17).

6. *Music.* How could we live without music? Stanley Chapple, the former director of the school of music at the University of Washington, has responded to that question: "For those who think we could get along without music, let them imagine what our world would be like absolutely devoid of music for just one week." That would be sheer cruelty! How much richer is life because of Beethoven's knocking motifs, Mozart's delicate tracery, and Brahm's sweeping themes. The poetry of the church has been wed to glorious music to give us memorable hymns. Even the quiet mood music we play on the stereo for dinner has its service. Don't forget to thank God for music.

7. *Nature.* How refreshing is a walk in the woods, a night spent in a cabin within earshot of the ocean roar, the Alpine flowers on a mountain trail, the varying moods of an evening sky or a lovely lake. In the surroundings of nature, simple recreation becomes true re-creation, whether on a week's vacation or five minutes under the night sky in your own backyard after supper. How wondrous a subject for thankful meditation is nature!

There are so many things for which to be thankful. Where does one begin? Where does one end? Let thankfulness be an intrinsic part of your daily worship time.

C. Dedicate Your Life and Possessions to God.

You have been given the gift of life so you might have the privilege of giving it back to the Giver. "You are a given man or woman," says Dr. Sangster.[3]

---

[3] W. E. Sangster, *Teach Us to Pray,* p. 22.

"... He who loses his life for my sake will find it," said Jesus (Matt. 10:39). That is a working principle of life. Dedicate yourself daily to God with as much fervency as if it were for the very first time.

If your life is so dedicated, it will be given to others. "There is no holiness without social holiness," said John Wesley. Indeed, one cannot be a saint in a vacuum; not once does the word *saints* appear in the singular form in the New Testament! One becomes a saint not only in private devotion but in the rough and tumble of dealing with real people in real life. Give yourself to persons. Do it with fresh enthusiasm every day.

But there is one hitch to this matter of dedication. We cannot make a full dedication of anything in and of ourselves; therefore, we must have the humility to ask God to bestow upon us the capacity to make that full surrender. By nature we are ego-centered; we simply are not about to lose our lives. In our most truthful moments we know we are afraid that we won't "find" them, even though Jesus promised this. Again, this fundamental weakness of our humanity must be turned over to God. Thus, the daily prayer of dedication sounds something like this:

> O God, I want to give myself to you and others. I really don't know how to do that, so in mercy reach down into my poor human heart and move me to total surrender. With a thankful heart I pray. Amen.

D. Seek God's Guidance.

The Book of Proverbs says there is security in an abundance of counselors (Prov. 24:6) and we know from experience that this is a workable rule. But such counseling takes time. So does the counsel of God.

If you do committee work, you know that your best decisions are hammered out carefully and slowly; if it is otherwise, calamity may be the result (if not for you, for the next generation living by the rule and tradition your committee too hurriedly established). So it is with guidance from God: Long-range guidance does not come speedily. It is slow, because God in his wisdom takes time to mold your thinking and adjust your inner being for the next step in his plan. Of course, some will not wait for that kind of guidance; but those who are willing to pray patiently will reap the rich results of a God-directed life (the real root of happiness), and know the quiet assurance of the divine will.

Some principles of guidance are laid down in the Bible. If prayer is a two-way street (God speaking to us even as we speak to him), the Bible is one way he has of getting through to us. For example, the Sermon on the Mount and the Ten Commandments are excellent guides to behavior; try living by these rules of conduct. It is a good idea to memorize the Ten Commandments (Exod. 20:1–17), parts of the Sermon on the Mount such as the Beatitudes (Matt. 5:1–11), Jesus' magnificent handling of the law and the higher righteousness of Christian living (in the remainder of Matt. 5), his injunction against practicing your piety before men (Matt. 6:1–8), and, of course, the Lord's Prayer (Matt. 6:9–13).

But what does one do when the Ten Commandments and the Sermon on the Mount (or other passages of Scripture) do not yield answers for specific occasions? Here you must learn the law of the inner voice. Individual guidance from God, received in prayer, is of vital importance. How easy it is to listen to your own voice pressing you to do the selfish thing! But it is the voice of God—the inner voice—you must learn to hear. The regular quiet time is the laboratory for developing that capacity to "hear." You will hear his voice in the busy course of the day, too. But it is in the stillness of the prayer closet that the gift of spiritual listening is given and received. God is always available in the instant of need to those who have made a habit of waiting quietly before him for insight and guidance.

Some principles of prayer guidance, then, are these:
1. Be quiet, patient, and open before God.
2. Be confident that he will communicate his wishes and help you execute them.
3. Let God speak to you through his Word, for in the Bible are laid down the rules of victorious living.

Mature Christians will be sought for counsel. Through a habitual prayer life, you will learn to distinguish your own

HOW TO PRAY: A SUGGESTED PATTERN

voice (and the voice of evil) from the voice of God so that you can give reliable counsel to others.

E. Make Intercession for Others.

Prayer or entreaty for others is called *intercession*. Its effect is immeasurable. Says Dr. Sangster, ". . . The great intercessors remain the men and women of secret influence in all communities, and to be mentioned in their prayers is incomparably more enriching than to be mentioned in their wills."[4] Sangster's statement assumes that prayers of intercession actually get results. And they do. This is not the place to discuss how they do; it is enough here to indicate that they do.

1. *The Need of Intercession*. Those most mature in prayer spend a large portion of their prayer time in intercession. The most obvious reason is the need of people about them. Just now these particular needs exist in one community . . . they are typical of any community at any time:

- A boy paralyzed from a trampoline fall needs God's help.
- A doctor's wife, recuperating from a difficult illness, needs complete restoration.
- A doctor's son needs salvation.
- An insurance salesman needs God and stability.
- A store operator needs to be born again.
- A missionary has become disillusioned.
- A father suffers from a broken heart because of his wayward sons.

. . . But this is only the beginning of a list that could be nearly endless. The needs are so great; the heartaches so real; the inner desire to pray so compulsive.

2. *Belief and Intercession*. "Praying Hyde,"[5] who saw so many souls saved as a direct consequence of prayer, learned that to praise God was a key to effective intercession. On one

---
[4] *Teach Us to Pray*, p. 29.
[5] See Francis A. McGaw, *Praying Hyde* (Chicago: Moody, n.d.) for the story of his prayer ministry.

occasion he began to pray for an Indian pastor: "O Father, thou knowest how cold—" But God said, "Stop." Hyde was commanded to see his fellow minister complete in Jesus, to see him as he would be when Christ had brought him into a full and vigorous Christian life. With this change of attitude, criticism was replaced by belief. John Hyde counted the things about this man's life for which to thank God. Subsequently the pastor's heart was set on fire; he had come alive to God.[6]

3. *Selflessness and Intercession.* We noted earlier that Jesus said, "He who loses his life for my sake will find it." That basic law of Christian existence proves true in prayer as in all other phases of life. The person who habitually centers his prayers on himself will soon be confined, lacking the outgoingness and expansiveness required for intercession. Even as our bodily organs (the eyes, for example) look out, so the spiritual organs are made to look out. To look constantly within is unhealthy as well as downright selfish. Ask God to meet your own needs—ask simply and straightforwardly—but spend the bulk of your time "looking out" on others. So subtly does self come back into the picture that even prayers of thanksgiving can focus on oneself. Stay away from undue attention to the self; cry to God for answers to the needs of the world! Sangster puts in this way: "Confession, thanksgiving, dedication, and the plea for guidance, keep the self very much in mind. Intercession carries us right away from self. As one glorious by-product of this secret intercession with God for others we have this lovely *un*self-centeredness, and prove once more that we never do anything for others which does not bless ourselves."[7]

4. *The Practice of Intercession.* When the inner voice of God directs you to pray for a person, give yourself in concentrated prayer for that person. You can do this while working around the house, walking to school, riding the bus to work, as well as in the more private prayer experiences. Allow yourself to think fully upon the one in need; talk freely to God about him, and listen with equal freedom to what

---

[6] Ibid., pp. 47–49.
[7] *Teach Us to Pray*, p. 28.

God may have to tell you about him. Sometimes prayers cannot be reduced to words; one simply stays quiet in the presence of God with the needy person in view. Let your whole frame and attitude focus upon the one in need; the cry of the pray-er's heart is, "O God, come to his rescue as you see best."

In the event of illness, focus upon the *person*, not his *disease*. You can make *yourself* sick by thinking too much about the illness itself. Positive, affirmative thoughts must dominate your prayers; negative thoughts are damaging. This is only another way of expressing the lesson John Hyde learned about employing belief instead of unbelief in prayer. Faith is nurtured in affirmation, unbelief in negative attitudes. Hold the difficult things up to the light of God's power; then watch him work out answers in his own way, which is frequently quite unlike yours. (It is an interesting fact that the people in the Acts of the Apostles were far more power-conscious than problem-conscious.) Then fuse the need of your friend with the power of God, and leave it there.

Intercessory prayer takes time, patience, a certain resting in God. When faithfully practiced, it gets definite results. It is moreover a major means of spiritual development for the one who prays.

5. *Short, Sudden Prayers of Intercession.* Not all of our intercession can be, or ought to be, of the concentrated type. Too many requests come to our attention. But there is what the theologian calls ejaculatory prayer—a short, sudden request lifted up to heaven in deep desire.

Harry, Bill, Mary, Jane come to your attention one after another. Good. Mention them one at a time to God, not too hurriedly, though you are involved in the day's work and cannot stop to think about each at length. The same principle holds true when going over your prayer list: not all names can be held in your mind at length. Your prayers must not be "sprayed," as it were; directing prayer too quickly and in too many directions results in no intercession at all, and drains your prayer energies. Yet ejaculatory prayers can be quite effective in the midst of a busy routine.

Remember that the prayer of faith can get more done in

a second than faithless prayer in an hour. Quality is more important than quantity (though sometimes quantity is necessary to produce quality).

F. Petition for Your Own Needs.

Relegated to the last place in our list of prayer functions is petition, though it certainly is not the least important. Petition is asking for ourselves. Clement of Alexandria believed there should be no petition at all. But Jesus taught us to say, "Give us this day our daily bread . . ."(Matt. 6:11a). He also told us to love our neighbors *as ourselves* (Mark 12:31), implying that he expects us to have regard for our own material needs. But we can easily become juvenile by focusing too largely upon ourselves; that is why we put petition in last place on our agenda for prayer.

The following humorous prayer illustrates how we can subconsciously slip into selfish praying: "O Lord, Thou knowest I have mine estates in the City of London, and likewise that I have lately purchased an estate in fee-simple in the County of Essex. I beseech Thee to preserve the two counties of Middlesex and Essex from fire and earthquake, and, as I have a mortgage in Hertfordshire, I beg of Thee likewise to have an eye of compassion on that county; for the rest of the counties, Thou mayest deal with them as Thou art pleased. . . ."[8]

We should avoid morbidity in our petitions. We can actually pray about our own problems so long and so hard that *they* become central instead of God. Some clever fellow has said that the existentialist's prayer is, "Give us this day our daily dread." It turns out that this is precisely what we pray for—though not in so many words—when we moan and groan over our problems at length. Take your needs to God, then leave them there in the confidence that God will bring his solutions in his own time and way.

---

[8] Quoted by Sangster, *Teach Us to Pray*, p. 13.

HOW TO PRAY: A SUGGESTED PATTERN

VI. EVENING PRAYERS: SUGGESTED PROCEDURES.

A. Give Thanks for Blessings of the Day.

Begin your evening prayers on the uplifting note of praise to God for his many blessings in the course of the day. Itemize your blessings in your prayer notebook. Here is a college teacher's list for a typical day:
1. Praise God for news of a school teacher seeking the infilling of the Spirit.
2. For a Mozart piano concerto heard off and on through the day.
3. For breakfast with my family.
4. For a crackling fire.
5. For dinner at home.
6. For a student who made her full surrender to God.
7. For another student seeking salvation.
8. For fellowship with colleagues in a Christian college.

And so the list could go on and on. In the course of every day there are actually more things for which to be grateful than can be counted. The old gospel hymn "Count Your Blessings" is full of truth. The counting of your blessings before bedtime will contribute to a better night's rest, too. The practice of the praise of God is healthy—physically, psychologically, and spiritually.

B. Confess Your Sins.

Have the courage to review your day with utter honesty. Ask, Have I wounded anyone today? Said a cross word? Been unkind in any way? Been dishonest? Even a little bit? Is there anything at all I must make right . . . by repayment or apology? Need I ask God's forgiveness for any misdeed or unrighteous thought?

Do not think so long upon your faults that you become a problem to yourself and God. That is not confession; it is unhealthy self-concern. But where there has been an unchristian act, beg God's forgiveness, ask for strength not to do it next time—then forget it.

C. Intercede for Special Concerns.

All earnest Christians have special or urgent prayer matters at all times. The objects of prayer shift with the passing days, as a rule; but it is imperative that we give ourselves to frequent prayer for those individuals God puts upon our hearts in a special way. Remember them before you go to sleep at night. Is there an unsaved young man in your community? Remember him in the evening. Is there a missionary friend in a war-torn part of Africa needing particular help just now? Remember her. Is there a relative especially in need? Don't forget him. The fact is that no prayer earnestly lifted up from the heart is wasted. God hears and answers every prayer. He does.

D. The Closing Thoughts of the Day Should Be of God.

Even as the first thoughts of the day should be of God, so should the last. Let *him* be the alpha and omega of each day.

> When the soft dews of kindly sleep
> My wearied eyelids gently steep,
> Be my last tho't, how sweet to rest
> Forever on my Saviour's breast.
> –John Keble

John Baillie was enamored of what he called "The Theology of Sleep."[9] He saw very clearly that the practice of the presence of God was not only a daylight affair; for the devout it continues through the hours of sleep. Baillie believed that prayer somehow continues "without ceasing" while we sleep. He commented, "Some of the saints have gone so far as to say that among the things God gives to his beloved in sleep is an increase in their love of Him."[10] Think

---

[9] John Baillie, *Christian Devotion* (New York: Oxford University Press, 1962), chap. 11, "The Theology of Sleep," pp. 71ff.
[10] Ibid., p. 74.

of it! Spiritual growth can continue even while we sleep! We can "wake up better men than [we] went to bed!"[11] If our leisure thoughts are habitually of God, if our closing thoughts of the day are of him, if the very warp and woof of our being cries after more of God, then it is clear indeed that God is at work in us twenty-four hours a day. What a lovely context in which to receive the psalmist's words, ". . . He giveth his beloved sleep" (Ps. 127:2).

FOR DISCUSSION

1. Summarize the reasons for making the first thoughts of the day of God.
2. Why is the early morning a good prayer time for many? Is it for you? Why or why not?
3. What is your reaction to the 15–10 program?
4. Study and discuss adoration (praise), thanksgiving, dedication, guidance, intercession, petition.
5. Discuss evening prayers. Thanksgiving, confession, and intercession play what part in evening prayers?
6. Why should the last thoughts of the day be of God?

BIBLIOGRAPHY

Baillie, John. *Christian Devotion.* New York: Oxford University Press, 1962.
McGaw, Francis A. *Praying Hyde.* Chicago: Moody, n.d.
Sangster, W. E. *Teach Us to Pray.* London: Epworth, 1951.

---

[11] Ibid.

3

HOW TO PRAY FOR REVIVAL

The revival we yearn for will come when we plead with God for it. Our prayer for revival must be a crying out for the salvation of the world in this hour of crisis; a crying that says, "Let my heart be broken"; a crying to see individuals saved from their sins; a crying that pushes our prayer thoughts out into a worn and torn world. When our praying is really that earnest we will witness an exciting change in the church and in the world.

I. REVIVALS ARE ALWAYS PRECEDED BY PRAYER.

"There is no known revival without . . . [a] prelude of prayer."[1] A. T. Pierson, well-known minister and writer, said, "From the day of Pentecost, there has been not one great spiritual awakening in any land which has not begun in a union of prayer, though only among two or three; no such outward, upward movement has continued after such prayer meetings have declined; and it is in exact proportion to the maintenance of such joint and believing supplication and

---
[1] W. E. Sangster, *How to Form a Prayer-Cell*, Westminster Pamphlet No. 10 (London: Epworth, 1958), p. 5.

intercession that the Word of the Lord in any land or locality has had free course and been glorified."[2]

Of the Korean revival of recent years, it is reported that missionaries began to pray daily at noon. The first month of noon prayers having ended, one of the men suggested that the meetings be discontinued because no revival had broken out. He was not only out-voted, but it was decided to spend even more time in prayer. This new prayer program continued for some four months. Then God poured out his Spirit; services of worship were broken up by confession of sins and weeping. In due course a great, sweeping revival came. Even the unbelievers who came to ridicule the revival were laid hold upon by God's Spirit and converted. Said a missionary, "It paid well to have spent several months in prayer: for when God gave the Holy Spirit, he accomplished more in half a day than all the missionaries together could have accomplished in half a year. In less than two months more than two thousand people were converted. The burning zeal of these converts has become a byword. Some of them gave all they had to build a church and wept because they could not give more. Needless to say, they realized the power of prayer. These converts were themselves baptized with the 'spirit of supplication.' In one church it was announced that a daily prayer meeting would be held at 4:30 every morning. [On] the first day four hundred people arrived long before the stated hour, eager to pray. The number rapidly increased to six hundred as days went on. At Seoul 1,100 is the average attendance at the weekly prayer meeting."[3]

A small group of elders met regularly to pray for revival in the Hebrides Islands to the west of mainland Scotland; that was the prelude to a movement of God's Spirit which continued many years. People are still being converted as a result of those prayers. "Praying Hyde" nearly lost his health

---

[2] Quoted in John Greenfield, *Power from on High, or the Two Hundredth Anniversary of the Great Moravian Revival 1727–1927* (Harrisburg, Pa.: Evangelical Press, 1950), p. 68.

[3] Ibid., pp. 91–92. Korean developments in the past thirty-five years document a continued spiritual awakening there. See John N. Vaughan, *The World's Twenty Largest Churches* (Grand Rapids: Baker, 1984).

and life praying at such length and with such intensity to see souls saved in India; the influence of those mighty prayers also continues to this day. Of the Welsh revival it is said that its two great waves—one in the last century, the other at the outset of our own—were preceded by little bands of earnest, praying people.

II. REVIVALS ARE PRECEDED BY PRAYER FOR PASTORS.

Your pastor is one of the busiest people in the community and thus needs the strength and support your prayers will bring. Occupied by a constant round of vastly varied activity, a minister's spiritual resources are easily drained. Your prayers for the pastor's regular spiritual renewal are solid help to that ministry. When the fires of revival burn in a pastor's own heart, the congregation will know it and begin to respond.

Says Armin Gesswein, "When God wants to talk to the church he talks to the minister. . . . It is difficult to usher revival into any church if the minister does not have it, and it is certainly almost impossible if the minister does not want it."[4] The pastor holds the key to revival. Pastors who have seen the touch of God's Spirit upon the lives of their people know that it comes from prayer—their own prayers and the prayers of others. Charles Spurgeon tells of a preacher who saw many souls won to Christ, but he "received a revelation from God that it was not his sermons or works . . . but the prayers of an illiterate lay brother who sat on the pulpit steps pleading for the success of the sermons."[5]

In the revivals in the churches of Norway in 1937–38, a notable example of awakening came in a downtown city church in Oslo. Before revival came, the prayer meetings in that church were all but extinct. The pastor was a discouraged man and nearly prepared to quit. Then he himself experienced fresh confrontation with the Spirit of God.

---
[4] Armin Gesswein, "Fire in the Church," *Decision,* March 1964, p. 4.
[5] Quoted by E. M. Bounds, *A Treasury of Prayer from the Writings of E. M. Bounds,* ed. Leonard Ravenhill (Minneapolis: Bethany Fellowship, n.d.), p. 88.

Subsequently his praying and preaching changed and, true to pattern, his people changed. They changed into concerned, praying people! Prayer meetings were now enthusiastically attended and the whole program of that church was infiltrated by a new sense of expectancy. In that context of expectancy the Spirit of God brought awakening—not just to the one city church but to other churches too.

Pray for your pastor! In all probability, that person is the key to genuine awakening in your own church and community. . . . But God can use another person as the special vehicle of awakening—namely, the evangelist.

III. REVIVALS ARE PRECEDED BY PRAYER FOR OUR EVANGELISTS.

In the 1800s there had been a revival movement in Wales. When it ended, some Welsh Christians prayed for another outpouring of God's Spirit. In answer to that prayer, God raised up a young coal miner who left mining to enter a Methodist school for the training of local preachers. He enrolled in February 1904, but shortly thereafter God called him to leave school and evangelize. Whereupon for eight months in 1904–1905 there was what one has called "in many ways . . . the most remarkable spiritual development of the twentieth century to date."[7] The movement spread over Wales and even a bit into England. There can be no doubt that earnest prayer caused it.

In preparation for the Los Angeles Billy Graham crusade of 1963, eighty thousand women prayed weekly; sometimes a prayer leader gave direction by radio. Each Graham campaign has had careful prayer preparation. I believe this is the chief reason for the many who have come to Christ in Graham meetings. For many years after 1949, when in Los Angeles the Billy Graham crusades got their "start," Mrs. Goode prayed for a special anointing of God's Spirit upon each team member. Willing to spend whole nights in prayer and fasting in order to see souls won to Christ, she literally

---

[6]Gesswein, "Fire," p. 4.

[7]Sherwood E. Wirt, "Bend the Church, Revival in Wales," *Decision*, February 1964, p. 8.

gave herself to intercession. ". . . Why not give yourself to prayer for pastors, evangelists and crusades?" asked Mrs. Goode of people who have time on their hands (cf. Luke 2:36–37, the story of the widow Anna, who prayed and fasted in the temple).

Will revival actually come? Armin Gesswein says in answer to that question: ". . . I used to hesitate, swallow hard, and breathe deeply in sighs. But I do not hesitate any more. My answer is, Yes, I do expect to see revival in the church and in the churches again."[8] Evangelist Gesswein is right; revival will come, indeed it is on its way because there is a growing number of God's people praying earnestly for our pastors and evangelists. Prayer is the real dynamic behind any religious awakening.

IV. WHAT WOULD REVIVAL DO?

W. E. Sangster has indicated ten definite results that would come from a genuine revival of religion:

A. Pay Old Debts.

First, says Sangster, revival would *pay old debts*. He observes that some people said the Welsh revival was mere emotional fanaticism until they found that "people were paying old and neglected and half-forgotten debts." When this began to happen, even with debts written off as quite "hopeless, they looked upon it as a miracle and they criticized the revival no more."[9] You see, real spiritual awakening is a very practical affair! Indeed, one of its visible results is that it will make people just plain honest. If you believe revival will do that, then pray for revival.

---

[8] Gesswein, "Fire," p. 4.
[9] W. E. Sangster, *Revival: The Need and The Way*, Westminster Pamphlet No. 7 (London: Epworth, 1957), pp. 1–2. All ten results of revival are given in this excellent pamphlet.

B. Reduce Sexual Immorality.

Second, Sangster says that revival would *reduce sexual immorality*. Dr. Sangster reviewed the morals of his native England and saw a desperate need for revival,[10] but what of our own country? The periodic survey of the American sexual morals given in *Time* magazine indicated as early as 1964 an alarming decline of personal purity in our own country. *Christianity Today* observed that the 1964 survey "describes in matter-of-fact detail this overturn in the private morality of millions of American youth and adults. It is not pleasant reading. . . ."[11] The unrestrained sex behavior of our country could well contribute to its downfall just as it did to the collapse of Rome and France. It is time we fell to our knees and cried to God for the return of a biblical morality. The late C. S. Lewis's last article dealt with this timely subject; in it he spelled out a rationale for the Christian teaching about sex and marriage, adultery and remarriage.[12] He came down hard on the side of the Ten Commandments.

A young man heard his pastor preach a pointed sermon on sin; it communicated to him precisely because he was living in sin—sexual sin. Convicted, he found his way to the minister's study at the close of the service, confessed his miserable sin, and proceeded to make right his living patterns. What had happened? The fact of his own sin had collided with God's righteousness; awakening came to his heart and mind; God changed him.

Who will doubt that such change is widely needed in our day? The broken homes, the illegitimate children, the mentally disturbed, the broken-hearted wives and mothers, the maladjusted children (and so frequently the maladjustment continues throughout life!)—all could be drastically reduced by the keeping of the simple biblical commands about sexual purity. Spiritual awakening goes a long way

---

[10] Ibid., p. 2.
[11] "Another Exposé of U.S. Morals," *Christianity Today*, February 14, 1964, p. 27.
[12] C. S. Lewis's, "We Have No Right to Happiness," *Saturday Evening Post*, December 21–28, 1963, pp. 10, 12.

toward bringing people to this true and workable ethic. Then pray for revival.

C. Reform the Arts and the Media.

Revival would *disinfect drama and the press,* says Sangster in the third place. As Sangster observes, the evangelical church does not quarrel with drama or literature as vehicles of communication. Thank God for any art form that contributes per se to innocent pleasure and effective communication. But how distorted, how warped, how demoralized have the stage and press become! Dramatists feel at perfect liberty to make light of sin in all its forms. In television productions it is the common thing, even on telecasts for youth, to show people drinking and killing. The situation is no better in novels—it is frequently worse!—in the name of "realism."

Moreover, the theater and movie advertisements of our daily newspapers use sexual looseness and horror as "come-ons." "Picture" magazines on our newsstands are highly suggestive; and even the filthiest can be purchased by teenagers. (*Christianity Today* ran an experiment a few years ago to prove it!) Pornography is a thriving business today. A revival of religion would change that.

Let us pause to thank God for the fine publishing houses across the whole Christian world that are set apart for evangelical purposes. Let us also thank him for the fine newspapers dedicated to nobler journalistic purposes. But the journalists and playwrights dedicated to high morals and nobler purposes are all too few. Then let us pray earnestly for an authentic awakening.

D. Lessen Divorce.

Sangster's fourth suggestion is that a revival would *diminish the rate of divorce.* It is no use reviewing the statistics—we are numbed to them these days—but what a godsend it would be to see that picture change. Riding a bus to California, I chanced to sit by a teen-age girl. In the course of the ride she revealed the miserable story of her marriage and—believe it or not for one so young!—her divorce. Her words ring in my ears to this day: "I hate divorce!"

Sangster is so right: ". . . the very texture of society gets flabby as divorce gets common. Young people actually enter marriage with their eye on the back door. 'Oh well, if it doesn't come off, there is always divorce.' "[13] You see, when people enter marriage with that attitude—as so often they do today—divorce tends not to be considered a moral problem at all. It is just another event. God help us! God send us a revival! God give us a revival of Christian marriage!

"Should I marry a divorced man?" asked a young lady. What do you say? A thousand facts and a hundred cases seem to flood across your mind at a moment like that. You can think of some couples remarried who have made it. But how many you can think of who haven't! They return for counsel again and again, and each time it is "the other person's fault." Neither awakening to self nor God has taken place.

But what if such awakening would take place? It happened to one young man; his pastor-counselor talked sternly and realistically. He came alive to himself, his God, and his moral responsibilities. He "fell in love" all over again with his wife!

Authentic Christianity remakes our homes! Then pray fervently for revival.

E. Reduce Juvenile Crime.

Dr. Sangster's fifth point is that revival would *reduce juvenile crime*. The trend in our country is well known; again, it will do little good to review the statistics. The apparent causes are fairly well identified. But the real solution to juvenile delinquency is the Christian home and community. With the advent of sound Christian faith, parents begin to shoulder their responsibility, while others develop a social conscience and begin to support community and church organizations for youth. With spiritual awakening, people

---

[13] Sangster, *Prayer-Cell*, p. 4.

see the imperative of strong holiness preaching, consistently heeded and practiced through the years of childhood and youth. It is all summed up in this: One will not be good unless "he *wants* to be good. Then he will be good in the dark."

"But what makes people *want* to be good?" asks Dr. Sangster. "Sound religion does it."[14] Then let us pray earnestly for a revival of godly living.

F. Relieve the Prisons.

Revival would *lessen the prison population*, says Sangster in the next place, and his argument is so persuasive that it needs our careful attention. He points out that in England the prison population is increasing. "Is it only a coincidence," he asks, "that the generation which saw the churches empty saw the prisons full?" Dr. Sangster gives a personal incident; he says a man denied that connection to him: "The churches have been emptying for more than a generation. Only of recent years have the prisons been over-full." "I know the answer to that," Pastor Sangster says. "The generation just past lived on the moral capital of its predecessors—a moral capital built up by the attendance at church, and respect for spiritual things. Now the capital is exhausted." Sangster observes that the exhaustion of moral capital may be more serious than Britain's loss of monetary capital, then continues: "The bill usually comes into the third generation. How often I have heard young people, going wrong, say in scorn of church: 'My parents were decent and they had nothing to do with church.' Was it any good pointing out to them that their parents were often living on the fine past of their forebears and that the account was now overdrawn?"[15]

Attendance at church lends support and undergirding to the very source of community and the moral fiber that keeps society orderly and people decent. The church exists to nurture us in religion which results in genuine godliness. Let

---
[14] Ibid., p. 5.
[15] Ibid., pp. 5–6.

us expose ourselves to it, nurture our children in it, lend our community influence toward it, and pray with unceasing energy for the expansion of it.

G. Increase Productivity.

Dr. Sangster becomes intensely practical when he says in the seventh place that revival would *improve the quality and increase the output of work.* In a recent issue of a leading American magazine, the question was raised, Is there too much leisure today? It pointed out, among other things, that some are spending too much time on the coffee break. This kind of cheating is a well-known phenomenon in our culture (some do it by having a work partner punch the time card in their absence!). Some rationalize it; others know it is quite wrong but do it anyway.

A revival of religion would do away with that sort of thing. People would become conscientious. They would be sharply aware that stealing time is surely not loving one's neighbor as oneself, that someone is suffering because of this carelessness. They would realize that dishonesty is the basic issue at stake.

"Real religion," says Sangster, "makes a radical difference to daily work. It does it this way. A man is taught that he does not work chiefly for wages, or the foreman, manager, boss, shareholders, state, or community. At the last, his work is rendered to God. He needs the wages, of course. The service of the community is a high expression of his chief loyalty. But his chief loyalty is *to God.*" Dr. Sangster brings his point home with pungency: "It is bringing God into it which makes the difference to work. It must be done well; it is *for God.* It must be done without clock-watching and time-wasting; it is *for God.* Frankly, not even love of country or the hope of making a bit more for yourself is a motive sufficiently powerful to overcome the inertia of our nature in days of high taxation. It calls for the steel and granite of deep religion. Men work to the uttermost who work for God."[16]

---

[16] Ibid., pp. 6–7.

H. Restore the Nation's Sense of Destiny.

Dr. Sangster's eighth idea is that revival would *restore to the nation a sense of high destiny*. He talks of course about his own country's problems. But what of ours? The 1960s were the decade of race revolution in America. What had lain dormant came awake; what had been smoldering erupted into flame. Considerable legislative reforms and landmark court decisions of the late 1960s and early 1970s helped to change many of the inequities that had existed in the United States since the colonial era. However, many of those reforms have eroded. Unemployment among blacks is still much higher than among whites because of outright prejudice in hiring practices and because of the persistent inequality in the education of whites and blacks. New immigrants from Latin America and the Orient are being treated with the same sort of discrimination once practiced toward blacks. So we now run the risk of losing our self-respect (and the respect of other nations) if we do not practice what we preach about "equal rights." America's high destiny is deeply involved in this issue.

America cannot come awake to its social responsibilities without the activity of God himself in individual human hearts. It is one thing to talk about equal rights, quite another to allow them to become a reality. It is one thing to preach justice, still another to put that preaching into practice. Legislation may help, but it won't turn the tide alone. What will get the job done? Honest-to-goodness religion. A real look at the Cross will soon to make one come alive to the truth that Christ died for *all;* a proper view of creation includes the knowledge that God made *everyone*. Man's heart cannot see these truths apart from the miracle-working power of God. To pray for revival is to pray for a heart like God's, a heart of real love.

I. Win the War of Ideas.

Dr. Sangster's ninth suggested result of revival is that it would *make us invincible in the war of ideas*. Those are his very words, and well chosen they are. He declares that "the real war behind the cold war is the war of ideas."

Sangster asks, "[is the] last explanation of the universe . . . spiritual or material?" Let a great group of first-rate minds, who are at the same time wholly alive to God, come to grips with this central issue. "Communism tries to satisfy man's cravings for a spiritual purpose by persuading him that there is none—that only materialism is real. But some people who profess to believe in the spiritual prove by their deeds that they also are materialists at heart."[17] These are the kind of "Christians," says Sangster, who don't really believe in Christianity, they just want to "use" it. "This kind of religion will not dam the Red tide [of communism]. It doesn't deserve to. Only real religion will do that—personal and utter dedication, sacrifice till it hurts, the spirit of Christ in the day-to-day contacts of life. The finest schemes fail on the selfishness of man. Christianity teaches a secret neither communism nor capitalism knows: *how to die to self.* The possession and practice of that secret would make us invincible in the war of ideas."[18]

J. Bring Personal Happiness and Peace.

Revival would *provide happiness and peace.* People don't look happy today simply because all too frequently they are not happy.

I recall visiting a fine middle-class church. Materially there was nearly everything money could buy. You know the kind of situation—a new church building beautifully decorated in tastefully chosen colors, candles on the altar, lapel flowers for the leaders of worship, and so on. . . . But the people did not look happy; they were sad, unchallenged, dead to the God of all joy. This unreleased congregation needed that "real religion" which "makes people happy, as happy as the day is long."

True Christians, says Sangster, "get up in the morning with brightness and go to work with zest. They have the

---
[17] Ibid., p. 8.
[18] Ibid., p. 9.

HOW ARE YOU PRAYING?

answer to all the dark mysteries of life—suffering, bereavement, death. Nor is there any particular mystery about it. Anybody who was completely sure that the world is in the hands of a good God could be happy. Not even hydrogen bombs tossed about by half-mad men can damage the throne of God."[19]

And peace. What about that? That does not come by political maneuvering. Peace comes from God himself, first to individual hearts. World peace can come only when world revival comes; because revival brings peace to individual persons, and persons make up our world. Then pray for the revival the world needs so desperately.

V. THE FELLOWSHIP OF CONCERNED, BURNING HEARTS.

Dick Halverson, a young converted actor, had gone to Wheaton College, then to Princeton Theological Seminary to train for the ministry. In 1942 he accepted a call to the First Presbyterian Church of Coalinga, California where he ministered for three years. During that pastorate he was given the gift of a concerned, burning heart. Here is the story:

Even though his work seemed to be going well, Dick found himself experiencing a growing hunger for more of God. He was also noticing that his ministry was not as fruitful as it might be. In the midst of this spiritual struggle, Pastor Halverson accompanied some of his Sunday school teachers to a training conference at Forest Home in the mountains of southern California. The second night of that conference proved to be the turning point in his life.

On the way to his cabin that night, he passed outside the leader's door. (The leader was Dr. Henrietta Mears.) "I was strangely prompted to enter and pray," said Halverson. "Though the cabin was dark, I realized there were others inside, praying. Not wishing to disturb them I waited outside for 10 or 15 minutes." Finally he went in and,

---
[19] Ibid.

walking across the room, knelt quietly beside an empty chair.

The room was perfectly still . . . then the Spirit led him to pray. Others prayed too, and Pastor Halverson, in telling the story, said, "God came down into that cabin."

He felt no radical change, but "God visited us in a way none of us had known before. There was weeping and laughter, much talking and planning."

"What is more clear from that experience," says Halverson, "is the fact that upon the hearts of us who were in that prayer meeting was laid a burden for the world and a worldwide vision that persists to this day. Through the years that vision has been fulfilled in many respects in detail as we saw it that evening; and the vision remains as fresh and vivid as ever to us."

On that night a great annual college conference was born, a conference that has meant the salvation and encouragement of countless youth. Also on that night, Dick Halverson wrote five pungent paragraphs of commitment which were to form the basis of "The Fellowship of the Burning Heart":

> Having come to a personal belief in the Lord Jesus Christ and realizing that the urgency of the hour in which we live demands the highest type of Christian Discipleship, I wish to unite with a band of young people offering themselves as expendables, with a vision of evangelizing the youth of the world for Jesus Christ in the shortest possible time.
>
> I Am Committed to The Principle that Christian Discipleship is sustained solely by God alone through His Spirit; that the abiding life of John 15 is His way of sustaining me. Therefore I pledge myself to a disciplined devotional life in which I promise through prayer, Bible study, and devotional reading, to give God not less than one hour per day (Psalm 1).
>
> I Am Committed to The Principle that Christian Discipleship begins with Christian character. Therefore I pledge myself to holy living, that by a life of self-denial and self-discipline, I may emulate those Christlike qualities of chastity and virtue which will magnify the Lord (Phil. 1:20, 21).

I Am Committed to The Principle that Christian Discipleship exercises itself principally in the winning of the lost to Jesus Christ. Therefore I pledge myself to seek every possible opportunity to witness in order that I may always be engaged in winning someone to Jesus Christ (Matt. 28:19; Acts 1:8).

I Am Committed to The Principle that Christian Discipleship demands nothing less than absolute consecration to Jesus Christ. Therefore, I present my body a living sacrifice, utterly abandoned to God. By this commitment, I desire that God's perfect will shall find complete expression in my life; and I offer myself in all sobriety to be expendable for Jesus Christ (Rom. 12:1, 2; Phil. 3:7–14).[20]

The spirit of these words is surely a result of the "baptism of fire" of which the Gospels speak. It is surely reflected in Acts 2:3, 4: "And there appeared to them tongues like flames of fire, dispersed among them and resting on each one. And they were all filled with the Holy Spirit. . . ."

John Wesley said his heart had been "strangely warmed" in that way, and he went out in the power of God to change England. Missionary Al Gould tells the story of a pioneer missionary to China who, before he had learned the language, found his heart so burning with concern to see souls saved that he walked the streets weeping, pointed to his heart, then up to God—that unspoken message communicated and people were saved! Dr. K. Oda of Japan has observed that evangelism committees are apathetic until their hearts are set afire by holy concern, and then there is no obstacle too great to set up the machinery for kingdom advance.

I recommend that you do two things to implement the ideas you have encountered in this chapter:

1. Pray for a concerned, burning heart. This is a gift of God. You cannot manufacture that kind of a heart within yourself; it comes from God. You must pray for it.

2. Once God has given you a concerned, burning heart,

---

[20] V. Raymond Edman, ed., *Crisis Experiences in the Lives of Noted Christians* (Chicago: Moody, n.d.), pp. 73–76.

sign your name to Pastor Halverson's creed of "The Fellowship of the Burning Heart." That will take a degree of courage and depth of commitment that only God can give.

FOR DISCUSSION

1. Why are revivals always preceded by prayer? Give examples.
2. Wherein is the pastor a key person for revival? What are your comments on the Oslo story?
3. List some reasons evangelists need our prayers for revival.
4. Discuss with another Christian each of the ten results of revival listed by Sangster.
5. Discuss the relationship of concerned, burning hearts to revival.
6. What do you think of Pastor Halverson's five paragraphs on "The Fellowship of the Burning Heart"?
7. Explain: Only God can give one a burning heart; a person cannot manufacture within himself this kind of concern.

BIBLIOGRAPHY

Edman, V. Raymond, ed. *Crisis Experiences in the Lives of Noted Christians*. Chicago: Moody, n.d.

Greenfield, John. *Power from on High, or the Two Hundredth Anniversary of the Great Moravian Revival 1727-1927*. Harrisburg, Pa.: Evangelical Press, 1950.

Ravenhill, Leonard, ed. *A Treasury of Prayer from the Writings of E. M. Bounds*. Minneapolis: Bethany Fellowship, n.d.

_____. *Revival Praying*. Minneapolis: Bethany Fellowship, 1963.

Sangster, W. E. *Revival: The Need and The Way*, Westminster Pamphlet No. 7. London: Epworth, 1957.

4
HOW TO ESTABLISH AND MAINTAIN A PRAYER GROUP

In this chapter we will consider the benefits of that fellowship of prayer known in our day as the "prayer group" or the "prayer cell." Some fellowships are made up of just two people, others of three or four, still others of ten or a dozen. These are the typical group sizes today, and it is interesting indeed that Jesus was involved in all three: John was his closest friend; Peter, James, and John were his three righthand men; the Twelve made up the full complement of the apostolic circle while Jesus was on earth.

Yet the size is not the important thing; the supremely significant factor is the presence of Christ himself. He makes the difference. Peter, James, and John were close because of *him;* the Twelve followed *him.* Friendships are established because of a common center of interest; Christian fellowship is unique in its common center, Jesus Christ.

I. HEARTS STRANGELY KNIT TOGETHER.

John Wesley said that the hearts of people who meet together for prayer are "strangely knit together." That must have been the experience of the early Christians. They ate together, worshiped together, prayed together; indeed, "those who believed were of one heart and soul" (Acts 4:32 NASB). The early church even shared their material possessions, which Thomas Kelly says was "only an outcropping of a profoundly deeper sharing of a Life. . . ."[1] This divine gregariousness is the gift of God; it is supernatural; it is a glimmer of the precious jewel called "fellowship." This strange knitting of souls together in God is characteristic of any true prayer group.

You should be able to sense when you have encountered a person who is truly living "in Christ." The conversation is not merely a passing-the-time-of-day sort of affair; it is communion and knowledge at a deeper level. Sometimes the knowledge comes with a strange immediacy, even though you have just met. You sense that rare bond of fellowship which draws people together; there are common interests, mutual concerns, and especially there is your common life in Christ. You cannot resist fellowship because there is an "insistent craving which will not be denied."[2] You are strangely knit together.

Common religious *activity* is not the secret of this deeper fellowship. Some people are engaged in the noblest of activities—some of whom are leaders in the church—who haven't entered into this intimate fellowship of prayer. They are admirable, they are efficient, they are experts in their respective functions; but you sense they are not part of the company of the committed. They may be orthodox in their theology and quite sincere in their theological convictions; but they are chilly in their theological pronouncements. They may be cultivated people who are good at conversation, poised, and pleasant to be with. But underneath their social graces something is profoundly lacking. That lack is frequently covered by busyness, a feverish activity. Yet that missing factor makes intimate fellowship an impossibility. The "knitting of hearts" just can't take place.

The *self* is the real problem, isn't it? When self is more important than Christ, it erects an impenetrable barrier to fellowship. Thomas Kelly spoke of "those who are still oriented about self, rather than about God."[3] While some

---

[1] Thomas R. Kelly, *A Testament of Devotion* (New York: Harper and Brothers, 1941), p. 80.
[2] Ibid., p. 78.
[3] Ibid., p. 80.

Christians suspect this self-orientation is the reason for the absence of deeper fellowship, for others, "tragic to say, the very existence of such a Fellowship within a common Life and Love is unknown and unguessed."[4]

That word *love* is the real key to breaking down the barrier that self-centeredness erects to genuine fellowship! Intimate Christian fellowship does not come about by a purely social encounter or by striving to develop better "human relations." But let the vertical dimension (God-to-man) be cultivated before the horizontal dimension (man-to-man) and notice the result. Once the self is lost in God's love, the man-to-man relationship takes on an entirely new perspective. Knowledge of one another is "in Christ" through *his* love. The revealing of his love leads to the revealing of his people to each other. When two or more hearts filled with Christian love come together, the fellowship is established; somehow it "clicks." This is the spiritual church within the physical church. This is the experience of hearts being "strangely knit together." Let us examine some biblical descriptions of such a fellowship.

II. BIBLICAL DESCRIPTIONS OF THE PRAYER GROUP

Matthew 18:20 reads, "For where two or three are gathered in my name, there am I in the midst of them." And the verse prior to that says, "Again I say to you, if two of you agree on earth about anything they ask, it will be done for them by my Father in heaven." Christ is present in the fellowship of the prayer group, in the person of the Holy Spirit. He promised that his Spirit would be uniquely present in a group of people with ready hearts and listening ears.

Jesus had instructed his followers to wait for the promised Spirit. They did: "All these with one accord devoted themselves to prayer, together with the women and Mary the mother of Jesus, and with his brothers" (Acts 1:14). And again: "When the day of Pentecost had come, they were

---
[4] Ibid.

all together in one place" (Acts 2:1). It is significant that Pentecost came upon a *group*, rather than upon solitary persons. It is clear that the Spirit of God works in the atmosphere of true Christian fellowship.

After Pentecost the early church continued to enjoy the presence of God in group situations. Acts 4:31 is a case in point: "And when they had prayed, the place in which they were gathered together was shaken; and they were all filled with the Holy Spirit and spoke the word of God with boldness." Again, in Acts 12:12 we have evidence of a group prayer fellowship. The scene is in the home of Mary, mother of John Mark, where "many were gathered together and were praying."

Paul suggested the formation of men's prayer groups when he said, "I desire then that in every place the men should pray, lifting holy hands without anger or quarreling . . ." (1 Tim. 2:8).

That the Spirit works in the group, then, is made clear from the teachings of Jesus, Paul, and the early church. And what of postbiblical times; did God continue to bless the prayer group?

III. HISTORIC AWAKENINGS AND THE PRAYER GROUP.

Not only is the prayer group described in the Bible, it is confirmed in church history as well. A. T. Pierson said that there never has been a revival of religion without social prayer. He is right! The Holy Club, which included George Whitefield and John Wesley (along with other devout students at Oxford), was a prelude to the Evangelical Revival of the eighteenth century, which in turn was related to the Great Awakening in America. A great nineteenth-century missionary movement was born in the famed "Haystack Prayer Meeting" of 1806, which was made up of Williams College students. In our own day, The Fellowship of the Burning Heart was conceived in a mountain cabin prayer meeting at which Henrietta Mears, Dick Halverson, and other earnest Christians were in attendance.

Go far back into history or come right up to the present,

and in every case of a movement of God's Spirit, group prayer is involved. This is why W. E. Sangster speaks with such urgency about the establishment of prayer groups. He calls for a "higher level of convinced, persistent, and corporate prayer." He observes that "something seems to be added to prayers offered in fellowship which is not available in the same measure to the same prayers offered by the same people in separation." Finally he says, "If—for every important reason which requires it—we want to see the Christian religion revived among us, we must study to multiply the number of prayer-cells (or prayer groups)."[5]

IV. THEN WHY DO WE DRAG OUR FEET?

House meetings and small groups for prayer and discussion were probably never more frequent in all of Christian history than right now. The social cup of coffee, followed by Bible study and prayer is very common in our time. Some think that today this type of prayer fellowship is God's chief method of winning the lost and nurturing young believers today. To the extent that is true, let us thank God for it!

But let's be honest with ourselves. The fact is that our earnest pastors plead around the calendar for church members to respond to serious prayer groups, yet they get a half-hearted response. "The idea of prayer as the highest privilege and chief occupation of the day sounds secretly silly" to most, says Dr. Sangster. But "if prayer is fellowship with the Almighty God of this universe, how can it be other than the chief business and privilege of every day?"[6] Prayer in a warm-hearted group is the highest form of fellowship; it is biblically and historically validated. Then why do we not respond to the kindly invitation of our Lord, "For where two or three are gathered in my name, there am I in the midst of them"?

Said a graduate of a Christian college, "Frankly, I miss the daily chapel. I need that stimulus to live the genuine

---
[5] W. E. Sangster, *How to Form a Prayer-Cell*, Westminster Pamphlet No. 10 (London: Epworth, 1958), p. 3.
[6] Ibid., p. 7.

Christian life." The most obvious place to get that kind of stimulus during the week is in a prayer group. He would do well to join one and become a habitual attendant. John Wesley's great spiritual awakening came in just such a group in the year 1738, long after his college days.

Just think what a bulwark against temptation group prayer really is! Just think of the planning, aspirations, and dreams that come to light in the group! Think of the burdens shared, the joys revealed, the courage restored!

But "the gates of hell prevail against us for lack of prayer. The Kingdom is impeded in its coming for lack of prayer. *You* could be of service to God, to the nation, and to the world, if you would form, or help to form, a prayer-cell. It might be the most useful thing you have done in your life."[7]

V. YOU CAN BEGIN A PRAYER GROUP

"It seems incredible," you say, "that *I* should be a leader in a prayer group." But think about it. First of all, do you believe that if the number of prayer groups were sufficiently increased there would be a great lifting of the spiritual tone of our world? Do you believe that another revival would be the result?

Do you believe that the world is in desperate need of another spiritual awakening? Indeed, an awakening of far greater proportions than the world has yet seen? Are you concerned to see the needy helped and brought to the Lord Jesus Christ? If your answer to these questions is yes, surely you will become involved in a prayer group.

Now that word *concern* is the key. That is the genius of getting things done in the kingdom of God. Without concern nothing is accomplished for God or your neighbors. But if your heart is genuinely concerned, wait before God until you have his mind. After that you will want to have a part in

---
[7] Ibid., p. 8.

starting a prayer group if none is currently active in your community. But how?

A. Rededicate Your Life to Christ.

You will need all the spiritual resources you can summon in the task of starting a new prayer group. Temptation and discouragement are sure to come. So gird yourself for the task by rededicating yourself to the Lord's service. This has an added benefit: It will be proof that you are actually willing to work for the Lord.[8]

B. Seek God's Guidance.

Pray definitely about joining or starting a prayer group. If there are several groups you could join, seek God's guidance as to which one. Not all groups are equally vigorous. A sleepy group may need your enthusiasm, or you may need the contagion of a lively group. If there is no group you could or should join, explore with God how you could start one. Seek to discern the first person you should approach about forming a prayer group. That person should be alive to God and eager to improve the spiritual life of the community, or at least have the potential for spiritual adventure. God will direct you to such a person.

C. Make the First Contact.

Arrange to visit with the prayer partner of God's choice. Have an unhurried cup of coffee together. Convey your own deep desire for more prayer, and the need you feel to share and pray with others. If your friend responds, set aside an hour to meet together in the coming week.

D. Don't Feel Pressed for Time.

When the appointed time comes, *make it a leisurely experience.* Uneasy clock-watching is devastating. (If the hour

---

[8] Both Sangster, *Prayer-Cell*, p. 9, and Robert E. Coleman, *Introducing the Prayer Cell* (Huntingdon Valley, Pa.: Christian Outreach, 1960), p. 15, suggest fresh commitment as the first step in starting a prayer cell.

is well chosen, a hurried sense will not be necessary.) Begin to get acquainted on the spiritual level. Learn to share with one another prayer requests—not just (or even mostly) your own, but especially those of needy people in the community. Learn, too, to share victories and to be thankful. Conclude your hour together with prayer, silent or spoken, preferably both.

E. Seek Others to Join Your Group.

After you have met a time or two or more, you will very likely wish to *add a third member.* This suggestion will probably come quite naturally. "... Say, let's include Joe" (or Jane if it's a ladies group; or Joe and Jane if a couples' group). If the group grows to more than ten or twelve, it should probably be divided.

VI. SHOULD YOU BE THE LEADER?

Maybe so and maybe not. Let this decision emerge from your conversations with the Lord and with your prayer partners. Members of the group may want to take turns leading. Or you may want to have one person provide an overall leadership with regard to the logistics of your meeting (arranging for matters such as who will fix the coffee next time), and appoint each member in turn to lead devotions. The devotional leader should encourage members to share prayer requests and ideas. Actually, the best leadership may be nothing more than a quiet concern that keeps the group active in a meaningful way. It is much better, in fact, if one person does not do too much talking. If the qualities of a good leader were summed up, they would be these:

A. Have a Desire to Pray With Others.

First, the devotional leader must be someone who *really wants to pray with others.* If you are beginning the group out of a sense of duty rather than real desire, others will sense your motives and will be indifferent to the idea.

B. Be Able to Encourage Attendance.

Second, the leader must be someone who *will encourage regular attendance by the various group members.* (Appointing one to bring the coffee, another the cookies, another devotions—these are some practical ways to encourage attendance.)

C. Be Concerned With People's Needs.

Third, the group leader must be someone who *is genuinely concerned about the needs of people.*

VII. IN WHAT SITUATIONS CAN PRAYER GROUPS THRIVE?

Prayer groups spring up in every type of surroundings, but let's look at five typical situations.

A. Plan a Family Prayer Time.

The family is the most natural group unit in our culture, thus a logical group to meet for prayer. If you would like to transform your family into a prayer group, pick a time when the entire family is present. At our house that is right after breakfast each morning. Five minutes is plenty, especially if there are little children anxious to get off to school and their attention spans are limited. Make prayer and the Bible central to the family prayer time. Plenty of picture Bibles, Bible storybooks, and family devotional aids might be used. Mary L. Miles, *Quiet Moments With God*[9] (which was written in the first instance for her own children) and Maud and Miska Petersham, *Joseph and His Brothers*[10] (beautifully illustrated) are examples. Design the whole experience for the children, letting them see the pictures, helping them read the Bible, and inviting them to make prayer requests, pray

---

[9] Mary Lillian Miles, *Quiet Moments With God* (Winona Lake, Ind.: Light and Life, 1957).

[10] Maud and Miska Petersham, *Joseph and His Brothers* (New York: Macmillan, 1958).

aloud, or participate in whatever they can. Whenever there are children in your family circle, the key to successful family prayer is *their* involvement.

B. Arrange a Noon Luncheon.

Hubert Mitchell made this kind of prayer group well-known in Chicago. Business and professional people brought sack lunches to a quiet office and shut the door to eat together, share their experiences, and have a time of Bible study and prayer. Mr. Mitchell believed this was an effective method of nurturing new converts; but of course it is practicable for older Christians, too. The noon luncheon plan could work in a variety of ways: at a restaurant (provided there is a quiet room available), on a university campus (in an empty classroom or dormitory room), or in an automobile parked in a factory parking lot. The possibilities are endless. Use the method that works naturally in your situation.

C. Schedule a Homemakers' Coffee Hour.

Such a group usually functions best in mid-morning, say about ten o'clock, when the children are in school. Meet in one of the homes, or in the church kitchen. You may find that the coffee takes up too much time and that your group is eager enough to get right at the business of sharing and praying. Some ladies' groups appreciate a guidebook such as *The Upper Room* magazine[11] or Rosalind Rinker's book on conversational prayer.[12]

D. Start a Men's Early Breakfast.

Perhaps at six-thirty, before leaving for work at eight o'clock, a men's group can meet without interruption or schedule conflicts of any kind. Have one man bring rolls, another a pot of hot coffee, another fruit or eggs, and one to

---

[11] *The Upper Room* (Nashville: The Upper Room, published quarterly).
[12] Rosalind B. Rinker, *Prayer: Conversing With God* (Grand Rapids: Zondervan, 1959).

bring devotions. Keep a rotating record of each man's responsibility for the meetings: it has the twin advantages of keeping everyone involved and preventing any one person from being burdened with too much responsibility. Leave enough time for prayer in each week's meeting; it is easy to let the time slip by with casual talk and breakfast preparations (therefore keep them as simple as possible).

E. Couples Could Meet in a Home.

Married couples occasionally need to get away from the demands of the home; one of the most constructive releases is the prayer group. Suppose three or four couples are interested in forming such a group; work out a rotating system whereby the group meets in a different home each week. Evening is the best time to meet, though it will be necessary—and sometimes difficult—to find an evening suitable for all to attend. Don't let occasional absences discourage the continuation of the regular meeting.

You may know of a better situation than one of the five above. Fine! The main thing is that the group is started and maintained. John Wesley was so completely convinced of the value of the prayer group (he called it the "class meeting") that he made it the foundation of Methodism. Whatever your time, place, and method of getting together, do it! It will be a major plank in your own spiritual development.

VIII. CONVERSATIONAL PRAYER.

The essence of Rosalind Rinker's concept of "conversational prayer" is simply this: Frequently we feel in the prayer group that we must say a little "speech" to God—or rather to the others present! Some may go so far as to figure out in advance just what to say. This, maintains Miss Rinker, can rob the pray-er and the group of the real benefits. To handle this problem, she suggests "conversational prayer," which is exactly what the name implies. One begins with a single sentence of prayer on a given subject, another follows right away with a sentence on the same subject, and others follow until that subject is exhausted. Then another member of the

HOW TO ESTABLISH AND MAINTAIN A PRAYER GROUP

group, sensing the time to shift the focus, begins with a fresh subject. That new subject is exhausted "conversationally." The process is repeated until the period of prayer is over. (The sensitive leader knows when the group is ready to end the prayer period.)

To try a new prayer procedure like this requires a willingness on the part of the group. If the prayer cell is glued to a traditional method, the different way will seem awkward. Indeed, if the older way is tried and true for your particular group, there may be no real need to change. But if vitality is lacking, or if a certain deadness has intruded, then give the new approach a try.

IX. NINE WORKING PRINCIPLES FOR PRAYER GROUPS.

A. Pray in the Spirit.

First, all praying in your group should be done "in the Spirit." John 14–16 gives us Jesus' prophecy of the coming of the Holy Spirit. In those chapters we see repeated the verses that promise "if you ask anything in my name I will do it." Note that this promise is given with reference to the Spirit; it holds true only when our asking has to do with the Spirit and his purposes. Praying "out of the Spirit" is to pray for *our* purposes, while praying "in the Spirit" is to pray for *his* purposes. On occasion your group may need to raise the question, "*Should* we pray for this or that?" The Bible, the inner voice of God's Spirit, and common sense will provide the answer when God chooses to give it and hearts are open to receive it. "On many issues, only quiet fellowship and conversation with each other and with God clears the mind" and gives him a chance "to shape His wishes in our hearts."[13]

B. Make Complete Preparation.

Take time to prepare your minds and hearts for prayer. Every change of experience requires adjustment, great or

---
[13] Sangster, *Prayer-Cell*, p. 13.

small. Most people cannot suddenly change their thoughts to those of prayer. It takes time to change or adjust to it, so take time. Quiet discussion, periods of unhurried silence—these aid the adjustment to any group prayer time. This procedure will create an atmosphere in which we can become aware of God's presence. Knowing he is really there is a key to knowing he will hear and answer your prayers.

C. Allow Periods of Silence.

Don't worry about periods of silence. The normal procedure in a prayer group is in all probability (1) the sharing of needs, then (2) volunteer prayers. So that no one will feel awkward (as in the case of one who has not prayed out loud very many times, or perhaps never), establish the ground rule that verbalized prayer every moment is not necessary. Encourage periods of silence. Corporate silence can be one of the most meaningful experiences of prayer and meditation known to man. E. Stanley Jones used it in his Ashram retreats to great advantage. (One meal was usually eaten in absolute silence, and early morning group prayers began with a half hour of quiet.) Perhaps you recall the story of Wordsworth and Coleridge spending an evening by the fire, without a word passing between them . . . until the evening was over, when one said, "It has been a great evening!" The communication of heart to heart is sometimes the richest kind of communication.

All this is not to say that verbal prayer should be discouraged. It is to be *encouraged*. The only point of this paragraph is that Quaker silence has its advantages, too; these are (1) the removal of the feeling of awkwardness or restlessness if no one is praying out loud, and (2) listening for the voice of God.

D. Make Your Prayers Others-Oriented.

Pray unselfishly. Bring into focus the desperate concerns of the people in your circle of knowledge, and praise God for answered prayers. Mention those who are ill and those who have been healed, those who need to be saved and who have been recently converted, those who have suffered bereavement and who have found solace. To pray for others in this manner is of incalculable service, so let the bulk of your prayers be in this others-oriented direction. Not that you should never pray for yourselves; after all, the prayer group is for its members, too. But the prayer cell that is self-centered sooner or later defeats itself like all self-centered groups and persons.

E. Prioritize Your Concerns.

Put first things first. Not everything can be discussed and prayed about; not everything *ought* to be. Cull out the prayer requests of highest importance (the Spirit and feeling tone of the group will generally make priorities clear). Concentrate upon primary, not secondary, matters. The need for world revival is, of course, our most urgent need.

F. Seek to Expand Your Faith.

Prayer always should stretch the horizons of your faith. Faith is a gift. We must be childlike enough simply to ask God for the gift. Once given, exercise it lest it atrophy; exercise it and see it grow. Believe God will answer your specific prayers; Jesus said, ". . . Whatsoever things ye shall ask in prayer, believing, ye shall receive" (Matt. 21:22 KJV), not *might* receive. John Baillie said reading stretches the mind a bit; likewise prayer stretches one's faith.

G. Pray Expectantly.

Watch for answers. Nothing strengthens faith so much as to see a real, live answer to prayer! Some prayer groups keep a record of what and who has been prayed for. By the same token groups could well keep a record of answers to those specific prayers. Then there would be documentary evidence that God hears and answers prayer.

H. Have Specific Concerns.

Pray about specific concerns more than general, ongoing concerns. To pray for Russia and America is good in its own way, but to come to specific cases is even better. Pray for the President of the United States, especially that he will be led of God in a definite current crisis. Ask God to strengthen the evangelicals in Russia (perhaps you know of a Russian pastor who needs prayer support). . . . When interceding about the sin of America, pray for the conversion of a specific troublemaker in your own community. . . . Whatever the subject of prayer, center upon definite issues, definite people, definite problems, definite causes.

I. Pray Persistently.

One of the truly fascinating principles of prayer is that it works for those who pray persistently. Who ever heard of a devout and faithful pray-er who doubted its value? True, not all the answers to puzzling questions about prayer will come to us in this life. God's silences constitute one of his great teaching devices; but more answers will come than we might suspect. The answers come not so much by "thinking them through" as by experience. Prayer is to be experienced more than explained. Someone has observed that the early church was not problem-conscious but power-conscious. Why? Because prayer was the daily life and breath of Christians in that era.

X. THE INDIVIDUAL AND THE PRAYER GROUP.

The Quakers use a warm and marvelous expression, "The fellowship of the concerned." A true prayer group is that, a fellowship of concerned people.[14] You are concerned about needs in your circle of knowledge, but you must also be concerned about each other. Thus, when one member of your group is ill, by all means show your concern by a call or

---

[14] This is one of Dr. Coleman's definitions of a prayer cell. *Prayer Cell*, p. 6.

a card. When one leaves the group "for no reason at all," a little love and attention might bring him back. Without permitting that debilitating self-centeredness discussed above, cultivate an atmosphere that makes possible the free sharing of your inner struggles and doubts. If you are to have perfect freedom to talk about things closest to your hearts, then it must be understood that what is said in this intimate circle is not carried outside it! To betray confidences can break up a prayer group. "He who goes about as a talebearer reveals secrets, but he who is trustworthy in spirit keeps a thing hidden" (Prov. 11:13).

XI. DOING THE TRUTH.

An Episcopal bishop has written a book entitled, *Doing the Truth*. The title is suggestive of an important principle of the Christian life, which has special significance for the Christian's prayer life. Prayer groups must put their good ideas, received at the kind hand of God through the circle of fellowship, into actual practice.

For example, one cannot be part of a lively prayer cell very long without coming to grips with the vital issue of witnessing. To talk about witnessing, even to pray about it, is one thing; but actually to witness is another. Ask God to teach you an effective method of witnessing and then to give you the people to talk to or be with. . . .

Or take the group (this is an actual story) that discovered their pastor could very possibly win a trip to Africa provided that just a little more money for missions was raised and the required notebook of local church missionary activities was compiled. The members of that prayer group parceled out the work, completed it in ten days' time, and made a long-distance call to the denomination's mission board office informing them that the requirements had been met. The result? The pastor took a never-to-be-forgotten trip and returned with a burning missionary zeal that will have a far-reaching impact.

XII. DON'T GROW STALE.

A prayer group can grow stale in several ways. One is by allowing a spiritual coldness to intrude. Another is by losing interpersonal rapport. If you sense your group drifting from a true God-centeredness, then work through W. E. Sangster's *A Spiritual Check-Up*. The booklet costs but a few cents; you may want to purchase enough copies for the whole group.[15]

If lack of rapport is the problem, you may be the only one who has isolated the problem, and very possibly you cannot talk about it freely. In such case, make it a matter of serious private prayer. Don't act until you have clear directives from God. Some groups might better disband than continue without that comfortable group feeling that is so important to free exchange. (If the only solution is to disband, then start a fresh group or groups.) But it is usually possible to repair the damage done and continue. It may be that someone is talking too much, that the group is "I-centered" rather than "other-centered," that the group has developed no service expression out into the community. Whatever the difficulty, pinpoint it under God's direction, discuss it when you can, and eliminate it.

XIII. RELATE YOUR PRAYER GROUP TO THE CHURCH.

Of course this doesn't mean that interchurch groups shouldn't exist. Sometimes there is great benefit in an "ecumenical" cell; this is one fine way to learn from each other, to profit from varied backgrounds. But even here the group ought to encourage a vigorous involvement on the part of each individual with his own local church. If the prayer group does not strengthen the church, there is something radically wrong.

How does the prayer group strengthen the church?

---

[15] W. E. Sangster, *A Spiritual Check-Up*, Westminster Pamphlet No. 1 (London: Epworth, 1952).

HOW TO ESTABLISH AND MAINTAIN A PRAYER GROUP

A. The Prayer Group Leads to Personal Renewal.

The prayer group should be an instrument to help people come alive to God. Let's face it, not every Christian is part of the "strangely knit" fellowship described at the outset of this chapter, not even every member of a prayer group. But the group can be the very instrument God uses to bring these people to a new level of spiritual commitment.

B. The Prayer Group Leads to Congregational Renewal.

A prayer group can also be an instrument to spiritually awaken an entire congregation. Every warm-hearted evangelist covets an active prayer group, knowing that the group prepares hearts for the Holy Spirit's work and that fervent prayers for revival bring results. "Every great revival has been preceded by periods of intensive, agonizing prayer. . . . The Welsh Revival of 1904-5" is an example. "The movement gathered in intensity until at last it burst into flame in the heart of Evan Roberts."[16] "The 1859 revival had no outstanding leaders at all! But—like all the others—it had the great prelude of prayer."[17]

C. The Prayer Group Builds Spiritual Enthusiasm.

It takes only one or two truly dynamic prayer cells to make the cell idea catch fire. Cells will multiply. The more groups there are (provided they are genuine), the livelier the local church will be. That is just a law of church life. Conversely, the fewer the prayer groups, the less lively will be the local church.

D. The Prayer Group Aids Evangelism.

The prayer group often becomes a method of winning the lost. When people begin to share and pray, the lost souls of the community sooner or later loom into their view.

---

[16] W. E. Sangster and Leslie Davison, *The Pattern of Prayer* (London: Epworth, 1962), p. 47.
[17] Ibid., p. 14.

HOW ARE YOU PRAYING?

A prayer group leader outlined his deep concern for witnessing. He was a young businessman, and he said with Paul, "Woe is me if I preach not the gospel." He explained, "My areas of obligation are (a) the customers who come into my store, (b) the wholesalers, (c) my fellows in Rotary Club, (d) business partners in the Commercial Club, (e) the local Chamber of Commerce. . . ." Nor was his a cold outlining of "duty"; rather, he was so fired, inspired, and filled with the Spirit that he meant it with all his heart when he said, "Woe is me if I preach not the gospel." That young man intended to see souls saved and make sure that his converts identified with a warm-hearted evangelical church.

FOR DISCUSSION

1. Is it always possible to find people whose hearts are "strangely knit together?" If not, should this stop you from having a prayer group? Would the group contribute to knitting hearts together?
2. Review the Bible passages supporting the prayer group idea.
3. Do you agree that an increase of prayer groups could lead to worldwide awakening? Why or why not?
4. What do you feel ought to be your own role in a local prayer group? Should you start a group? How will you contribute?
5. Why is *concern* said to be the key to prayer group leadership and participation?
6. Review methods of getting a group started.
7. In your view, what is the best procedure to follow during prayer group meetings? Do you think there is ever occasion for varying the accepted procedure?

BIBLIOGRAPHY

Coleman, Robert E. *Introducing the Prayer Cell.* Huntingdon Valley, Pa.: Christian Outreach, 1960.

Kelly, Thomas R. *A Testament of Devotion.* New York: Harper and Brothers, 1941.

Rinker, Rosalind B. *Prayer: Conversing With God.* Grand Rapids: Zondervan, 1959.

Sangster, W. E. *How to Form a Prayer-Cell.* London: Epworth, 1958.

─────, and Leslie Davison. *The Pattern of Prayer.* London: Epworth, 1962.

5

HOW TO UNDERSTAND THE TEACHING OF THE BIBLE ON PRAYER

If we are to progress in our understanding of prayer, we must study the Bible. If we are to overcome "emotional unreality" in prayer, we must get our feet more solidly upon the Word of God. If we are to avoid spiritual pride "because I pray so much" or "so well," we must study Jesus' teaching on prayer. Such a study will humble us.

What is the teaching of the Bible on prayer? In the brief space of this chapter I cannot hope to give anything like a complete answer; but perhaps I can provide some biblical keys to unlocking the treasures of prayer.

I. THE BIBLE TEACHES THAT THE POWER OF PRAYER IS UNLIMITED.

Jesus made the most astonishing promise: ". . . I tell you, whatever you ask in prayer, believe that you receive it, and you will" (Mark 11:24). The apostle John took this seriously and said, "We receive from him whatever we ask . . ." (1 John 3:22a). He is of course quick to spell out the conditions of this promise: "If our hearts do not condemn us, we have confidence before God" (1 John 3:21); "We receive from him whatever we ask, because we keep his commandments and do what pleases him" (v. 22b); "All who keep his commandments abide in him . . ." (v. 24). It is essential to keep these conditions clearly in mind, more important to abide by them. It would be a strange thing indeed for one to make a request of God when that person had no intention whatever of turning from sinful ways!

There are other conditions, too, especially the prerequisite of praying in the will of God. We should strive to know the relation of his will to our own good and the good of others who are affected by our lives. Yet in the economy of God there are some things we simply cannot know, and this accounts for some prayers being answered in the negative.

Having noted these warnings and conditions to Jesus' promise to answer prayer, Christians believe that the promise still stands. Thus we can have full confidence that Jesus will answer all of our prayers in a way that will accrue to our greatest benefit.

However, it is imperative to recognize that Christians are influenced by the near-universal doubt of our age. If we are honest, we must admit that we are not always sure that God does answer our prayers. Indeed, when prayers are answered, we are prone to find "reasons" why the consequences would have fallen into the shape they did anyway. We forget Jesus' admonition to extend our faith to believe quite openly that God does in fact hear and answer our prayers. Jesus would not have made such a promise if it were not true. Ask the person who prays faithfully; there is no doubt in that veteran's mind that the power of prayer is unlimited.

II. THE BIBLE TEACHES THAT PRAYER MUST BE IN THE NAME OF JESUS.

Listen to the specific statements of Jesus with regard to offering prayers in his name:

- "Whatever you ask *in my name*, I will do it. . . ." (John 14:13).
- "If you ask anything *in my name*, I will do it" (John 14:14).
- "You did not choose me, but I chose you and appointed you that you should go and bear fruit and that your fruit

should abide; so that whatever you ask the Father *in my name*, he may give it to you" (John 15:16).

- "... If you ask anything of the Father, he will give it to you *in my name*" (John 16:23).
- "Hitherto you have asked nothing *in my name;* ask, and you will receive, that your joy may be full" (John 16:24).
- "In that day you will ask *in my name* . . . ." (John 16:26).

It is clear enough that Jesus expects his followers to pray in his name. Why? God is in Christ; therefore, the very name of Christ stands for God. To say the phrase, "in Jesus' name," at the close of a prayer is not just a form, it is a concrete recognition that Christ is God. Further it is a recognition that there is spiritual power in Jesus' name.

The Book of Acts is full of evidence that there is power in Jesus' name: salvation is in his name (Acts 2:21); baptism is in his name (2:38); divine healing is in his name (3:6); authoritative teaching is in his name (4:18); gospel preaching is in his name (5:40); Christian suffering is in and for his name (5:41); missionary outreach is in his name (9:15); boldness is in his name (9:27); demons are cast out in his name (16:18); prayer is in his name (22:16). There is power in the name of Jesus.

There is yet another reason we pray in his name. He is our High Priest who "always lives to make intercession" for us (Heb. 7:25). A priest is one who mediates or speaks for another; even as we sometimes need another to assist in making an important contact, so Christ exists to contact God for us. He is our very personal High Priest. More, the Bible announces that he "holds his priesthood permanently, because he continues for ever" (Heb. 7:24). So it is in the name of our Mediator, Jesus Christ, that we make our prayers.

III. THE BIBLE TEACHES THAT TRUE PRAYER IS "IN THE SPIRIT."

Here is one man's experience of praying in the Spirit, that of the sainted Samuel Chadwick:

Early in the year 1882 there came to me an experience that lifted my life to a new plane of understanding and of power. I received the gift of the Holy Spirit. I was led in ways I did not know, for I had hardly so much as heard that such an experience was possible. The demands of an impossible task awakened me to a sense of need. I had neither power nor might in either service or prayer. I began to pray for power for service, and God led me to the answer by way of equipment for prayer. It was a great surprise to me, for I thought I knew how to pray, and had prayed much over the work to which He had sent me. When I began to seek power, my ears were opened before my eyes began to see. I heard testimonies to which I had been deaf. Others had been driven to God baffled by lack of power, but they always associated the gift of power with an experience of holiness about which I was not keen. It was power I wanted. I wanted power that I might succeed, and my chief concern for power was the success it would bring. I wanted success that would fill the chapel, save the people, and bring down the strong fortifications of Satan with a crash. I was young, and I was in a hurry. Twelve of us began to pray in band, and the answer came by

> A way no more expected,
> Than when His sheep
> Passed through the deep,
> By crystal walls protected.

He led us to Pentecost. The key to all my life is that experience. It awakened my mind as well as cleansed my heart. It gave me a new Bible and a new message. Above all else, it gave me a new understanding and a new intimacy in the communion and ministry of prayer; it taught me to pray in the Spirit.[1]

It is true! One's prayer life is radically changed after the baptism of the Spirit. Indeed, altogether changed. One looks back on the days before his Spirit baptism and wonders if there was any prayer at all. Of course there was, but somehow not prayer in depth, at least not very often. The difference is the Spirit within, helping us in our human

---

[1] Samuel Chadwick, *The Path of Prayer* (London: Hodder and Stoughton, 1931).

HOW TO UNDERSTAND THE TEACHING OF THE BIBLE ON PRAYER

"weakness" (Rom. 8:26a). The world of the Spirit comes alive; what was hidden is now visible, what was in bud is now in bloom. This in the fuller sense is what the Bible means by coming from death unto life (1 John 3:14).

Paul tells us that we do "not know how to pray as we ought" (Rom. 8:26b). Fortunately he does not leave us in this miserable situation; he assures us that "the Spirit himself intercedes for us with sighs too deep for words" (Rom. 8:26c). ". . . With groanings which cannot be uttered," is the classic phraseology of the King James Version. J. B. Phillips expresses the experience perfectly when he translates it like this: ". . . His Spirit within us is actually praying for us in those agonizing longings which never find words." The New English Bible also renders it helpfully: "We do not even know how we ought to pray, but through our inarticulate groans the Spirit himself is pleading for us, and God who searches our inmost being knows what the Spirit means, because he pleads for God's own people in God's own way. . . ."

Paul continues his discussion of praying in the Spirit: "The Spirit intercedes for the saints according to the will of God" (Rom. 8:27b). The Spirit breathes into our hearts those intercessions that he knows need to be lifted up to God. The Spirit is the great guiding, energizing force of prayer within lively Christians. He not only tells us for whom to pray; he *helps* us to intercede for them. "That," said Samuel Chadwick, "is the New Testament explanation of prayer that prevails. Though I did not know it until years after, that is what happened to me when God gave me a new understanding, a new joy, and a new power in prayer. A new Personality entered a new Temple, and set up a new Altar. As I live, yet not I; so I pray, yet not I. . . . The Spirit in my spirit prays."[2]

Genuine prayer could be no other way. We simply "do not know how to pray as we ought" (Rom. 8:26). We have desires, but how do we know that their fulfillment would be

---
[2]Ibid., p. 58.

in the best interests? The faithful Spirit takes our desires, molds them, and rechannels them for God's holy purposes.

There is another aspect to this great fact of the Spirit praying in and through us in our infirmities. A homemaker said, "Frankly, I couldn't pray too well today; I have been ill and have little strength." But even in our physical weakness, in our illness, God himself prays in the Spirit-filled Christian. "... When we feel even too weak to pray, we can rest confident that a divine Intercessor, a Helper, a Comforter, is voicing the longings we lack strength to express."[3]

Then there are times when prayer is "unuttered and unexpressed." One is in the presence of God, and that is enough. There is a sense of concern, of urgency, and of intercession, but no verbal expression. There is identification, unification, and communion. But no words. The deepest in prayer cannot be reduced to words; it is bigger than words. Perhaps the moments of most effective intercession are not when we are the most fluent, but when we are the most silent; not when we are the most expressive, but when we are the most adoring; not when we are the most demanding, but when we are the most cooperative.

IV. THE BIBLE TEACHES THAT CHILDREN ARE TO PRAY TO THEIR FATHER.

"Pray then like this," said Jesus, "Our Father ..." (Matt. 6:9). Jesus saw that true communion is a family affair. We are the church, which is the family of God; thus we are his children, and children address the head of their family as Father. Jesus wanted to make very sure that the relationship was personal, warm, satisfying, as in the case of a small child who is unself-consciously absorbed in conversation with his father. The child asks out of his heart of need; he asks for what he wants. He is not afraid; he simply asks. So it was that Jesus said very straightforwardly, "Ask, and it will be given you; seek and you will find; knock, and it will be opened to you, for every one who asks receives, and he who

---

[3] Charles R. Erdman, *The Epistle of Paul to the Romans* (Philadelphia: Westminster, 1925), p. 93.

seeks finds, and to him who knocks it will be opened. . . . If you then, who are evil, know how to give good gifts to your children, how much more will your Father who is in heaven give good things to those who ask him?" (Matt. 7:7-8, 11).

God the Father is approachable as well as transcendent (beyond us). Too great familiarity with God would cloud his majesty. He is both near and far away in order to command respect. Human fathers should be that way. They should be available, yet command honor from their children; they should be giving, yet not giving so much that they spoil their children. The spoiled child has no respect for his father. By the same token, if God were to give us on the spot every little thing we ask, we would be "using" him, instead of allowing him to use us. We are his servants, not the other way around. Jesus saw very clearly the majesty of God when he said, "My Father . . . is greater than all . . ." (John 10:29). To catch a glimpse of that greatness of God is to know his immense holiness. To be in his presence is to be in the presence of a King. We dare not be "familiar" with God; he is Father. He is "our Father."

God the Father understands us. He knows our innermost needs. "And in praying do not heap up empty phrases as the Gentiles do; for they think that they will be heard for their many words. Do not be like them, for your Father knows what you need before you ask him" (Matt. 6:7-8). The point is clear enough: When we ask something of an earthly father, we need not necessarily repeat the request over and over again; he hears the first time. By analogy, we know the same must be true of our heavenly Father. (If there is much repetition to the heavenly Father, it is perhaps because the pray-er is clarifying the issue in his own mind or being readied for the answer.) Jesus says that the Father knows what we have need of even before we ask. That is not to say we needn't ask. An earthly father frequently knows our needs in advance, too, but the very process of asking establishes a love relationship. The act of requesting carries its own benefits.

"But when you pray," said Jesus, "go into your room and shut the door and pray to your Father who is in secret; and your Father who sees in secret will reward you" (Matt.

6:6). Here Jesus has been talking about hypocritical piety (Matt. 6:1–15), contrasting it to genuine spirituality. We do not pray to be noticed by other people (that is pride which is the sin of sins); rather, we pray to be heard of God. Communion with the Father is the real objective. Think of that for a moment. If our verbal prayers are uttered for the "sake of the others," is that really prayer? It is prayer only to the extent that one is sincerely talking to God. Only that real, genuine talking to God is rewarded of God. God responds to the sincere prayer.

Next, think of praying in secret. The necessity of the regular quiet time has been treated elsewhere; here it need only be said that to be alone in the presence of God permits unhampered holy communication. Quiet solitude allows you to talk intimately, as well as listen and hear his voice. "It is quite natural," said Dean Inge, "and inevitable that if we spend sixteen hours daily of our waking life in thinking about the affairs of the world, and five minutes in thinking about God . . . this world will seem two hundred times more real to us than God." Pray in secret to your Father, admonished Jesus.

Listen to the further words of Jesus about the Father: ". . . I honor my Father. . . . Yet I do not seek my own glory . . ." (John 8:49–50). When we pray we dare not accept any glory for answered prayer; that belongs to God who did the answering! How difficult it is to give honor where honor is due. We so love to take it to ourselves, so ego-centered are we. But the Bible is replete with the doctrine of the glory of God. It is replete, further, with the doctrine that when you or I take God's glory to ourselves we sin. The consequences of the "pride of life" are inevitably tragic. Therefore, when we pray and God answers prayer, we are to stand back and look in "wonder, love, and praise" to the Father. Of Abraham, it is said that in anticipation of Sarah's promised child "he gave glory to God" (Rom. 4:20).

V. THE BIBLE TEACHES US TO PRAY WITH IMPORTUNITY.

In Luke, the Gospel of prayer, is recorded the parable of the unjust judge (18:1–8), in which a widow persists in

HOW TO UNDERSTAND THE TEACHING OF THE BIBLE ON PRAYER

presenting her case to the judge—to the extent of bothering him—until he responds by promising to "vindicate her, or she will wear me out by her continual coming" (v. 5). Luke also records the parable of the importunate friend at midnight (11:5-13), who persistently urged his friend to get out of bed and loan him some bread so that he might feed an unexpected guest. "I tell you," said Jesus in relating the story, "though he will not get up and give him anything because he is his friend, yet because of his importunity he will rise and give him whatever he needs" (v. 8).

Are these stories realistic portrayals of how God answers our prayers? Is God really that deaf to our pleas? Or is he reluctant? Surely God is neither. Why then did Jesus tell us to pray importunately?

Well, Jesus himself prayed importunately. His long prayer periods make that clear (Matt. 14:23, 25; Mark 1:35; Luke 5:16; et al.). The writer to the Hebrews says, "In the days of his flesh, Jesus offered up prayers and supplications, with loud cries and tears, to him who was able to save him from death, and he was heard for his godly fear" (5:7). In the Garden of Gethsemane Jesus prayed the same prayer three times (Matt. 26:44). Luke says of Jesus in the Garden, "And being in an agony he prayed more earnestly; and his sweat became like great drops of blood falling down upon the ground" (Luke 22:44).

In the history of the Christian church there have been many who agonized in prayer, who prayed importunately. Francis of Assisi used to pray all night on occasion. John Fletcher, sainted follower of John Wesley, set aside one whole night each week for prayer and fasting. Of John Hyde it is said that he almost lived on his knees.

But why? Doesn't God hear the first time? If our heavenly Father knows what we need even before we ask, why the prayer of importunity?

Prayer is like a coin; it has two sides. On one side are the words, "Ask and it shall be given you" (Matt. 7:7a); on the other, "Jesus offered up prayers and supplications, with loud cries and tears" (Heb. 5:7). Prayer is as simple as asking; but it is also work. At one time it is the quick breathing of a petition; another time it is accompanied with heavy sighs and tears. It is in point of fact a paradox. And to view exclusively one side of the paradox is to miss the other side of prayer. To ask and go on your way in faith is quite all right in some circumstances; in others prolonged labor is required until one has "prayed through." The full-orbed doctrine of prayer cannot possibly be construed as easy believism.

The Spirit within guides us in the shortness or longness of our prayers, in the immediate or delayed sense of satisfaction and faith. In all this, God is working out his program for our lives; something is happening to *us* in the very process of prayer—maturation. The hour of testing is the hour of growth.

We should admit also that there is a deep mystery to prayer (any paradox is mysterious). Let's just face the fact that we will never fully understand it. The importunate prayer is only one facet of the whole doctrine we cannot comprehend fully.

And while we admit the inexplicable nature of prayer, let us affirm its workability. A Christian worker tells the story of securing the largest number of children in the history of vacation Bible school for her local church. But in the midst of her "success," she wakened to the sobering truth that not a single child had been converted. She now came early each day, went to the church kitchen, and prayed for her Bible school children by name. This pattern of importunate prayer she followed religiously; the result was the salvation of many boys and girls.

VI. THE BIBLE TEACHES THAT GOD REWARDS THE EARNEST PRAY-ER.

Jesus said, ". . . Your Father who sees in secret will reward you" (Matt. 6:4b). What is the nature of that reward? What form does it take? First of all, the reward is God himself. "For where two or three are gathered in my name, there am I in the midst of them" (Matt. 18:20). What greater reward is there than that? What more satisfying recompense? To have God—that is the height of human experience. It is no wonder the psalmists repeat the command to "wait on the LORD"! To wait on him is to be in his presence. When you are frustrated, seek God; when weary, find God; when nonplussed, get God. He is your chief reward.

From this fundamental experience of God himself comes all of the other authentic rewards of prayer. The discovery of oneself, one's true self, comes in prayer. The finding of God's ultimate will for our lives is a result of divine contemplation. And then prayer brings power. It was so at Pentecost. "All these with one accord devoted themselves to prayer, together with the women and Mary the mother of Jesus, and with his brothers" (Acts 1:14). That was the Upper Room setting just before the descent of the Holy Spirit in power. The result? "And suddenly a sound came from heaven like the rush of a mighty wind, and it filled all the house where they were sitting. . . . And they were all filled with the Holy Spirit . . ." (Acts 2:2, 4). Fervent prayer somehow releases the power of God in the world. Just how this happens is not fully known, nor does it need to be fully known; it is enough to know the fact of released power. Said E. M. Bounds, " 'The effectual, fervent prayer' has been the mightiest weapon of God's mightiest soldiers."[4] Tennyson said, "More things are wrought by prayer than this world dreams of." This is no idle statement; it has become classic precisely because it is true. Let us fix in our thinking once and for all that prayer is not mere pious lip service, something Christians "do." No! Prayer is the mightiest force in the world. James 5:16 is as solid as the Rock of Gibraltar: "The prayer of a righteous man has great power in its effects." J. B. Phillips's translation reads, "Tremendous power is made available through a good man's earnest prayer." The simplicity and economy of words in the New English Bible is worth noting: "A good man's prayer is powerful and effective." If anyone doubts that, let him read the life of George Müller!

Do we hope for the winning of the lost? Prayer is a big chunk of the answer. "Nothing would turn the nation back to God so surely and so quickly as a Church that prayed and prevailed. The world will never believe in a religion in which

---

[4]E. M. Bounds, *Power Through Prayer* (Chicago: Moody, n.d.), p. 36.

there is no supernatural power. A rationalized faith, a socialized Church, and a moralized Gospel may gain applause, but they awaken no conviction and win no converts."[5]

Do we long for the burning heart? That passion which makes us channels of his grace? The fervently praying Christian knows what it is to have a flaming heart. John Wesley was up at four A.M., preached at five, and was in the saddle at six. He had a flaming heart kindled daily at the throne of grace. Francis Asbury traveled more miles on horseback than Wesley himself (Asbury traveled six thousand miles a year). He was a man of unremitting prayer. John Hyde saw hundreds brought into the kingdom and established a Deeper Life conference in India. His historic nickname, "Praying Hyde," makes clear the source of his power.

"I was ready to quit college," said Carol. "I just couldn't master the art of discipline, I couldn't study. Then one evening I heard Dr. 'Bob' Smith of Bethel College preach on making Christ the Lord of your life. While he was preaching, it occurred to me that Christ could become Lord of my study habits." And that is precisely what happened to Carol! In a moment of insightful prayer she received the gift of discipline. She is radiantly changed, for her study patterns are rooted in God. He is her power to study diligently and successfully.

But what of the life that seems to be just "ordinary"? "Nothing great ever seems to happen to me," said a dedicated church worker. "The great things are always happening to other people." This common attitude suggests the need of a word of caution: We tend to hear about all the "great" people and the "great" miracles. And that emphasis on spiritual greatness has its place; God permits us this knowledge to help us realize that he invades lives powerfully. We need to hear of "Praying Hyde," Hudson Taylor, William Bramwell, and the other mighty people of prayer. Their stories prove God's supernatural power. But what of

---

[5] Chadwick, *Path of Prayer*, pp. 87–88.

the loyal pray-er who just goes on apace, whose experience is undramatic and quite ordinary?

Samuel Chadwick rightly said, "The prayer-life in which there are no miracles may be the greatest miracle of all."[6] What did he mean? The gift of faithfulness day after day, with no great dramatic happening to command and demand other people's attention—that is a gift the world desperately needs, and it is a miracle (though not always recognized as miraculous). It so happens that the faithful church worker who said, "Nothing great ever happens to me," is one of the most usable instruments of God some people know. If she is not always "recognized" by man, she is by God. She is a woman who puts her prayers into deeds of lovingkindness and definite accomplishment. I would guess that better than ninety percent of kingdom work is done through ordinary praying people. The accomplishment of the work is the reward, and sometimes we live so close to that reward that we cannot see it.

Or take those who spent (or spend) hours in prayer. That is a very great gift, but not all Christians have it. Mrs. Billy Graham admits that "I do most of my praying 'on the hoof.'" She says that sometimes a busy homemaker simply cannot get down on her knees to pray. "But to know that you can wash dishes, iron, clean, shop, drive, and in whatever you have to do Jesus Christ is there beside you, urging you to talk over your problems with him—that is a joy and a comfort it is impossible to describe." She goes on to say that if a certain difficulty is not surmounted, "he helps you to face it and to go through it and to learn from it."[7]

Whatever your gifts in prayer, whatever your method of prayer, so long as the method is born of God it is rewarded. That is the promise of our Lord who is the highest authority known to the Christian. And let it be repeated with emphasis that whether you are seeing the "great" miracles or not, if you are faithful in the performance of your God-given assignments (homemaking, business, teaching Sunday

---

[6] Ibid., p. 97.
[7] Ruth Bell Graham, "Mercy Suits Our Case," *Decision,* April 1964, p. 9.

school, or whatever), you have your reward both in this life and the next.

VII. THE BIBLE TEACHES US HOW TO ASK.

Samuel Chadwick, in his classic book, *The Path of Prayer*, gives seven biblical steps in asking:

A. Simply Ask.

The promises in God's Word are legion. For example, "If any of you lacks wisdom, let him ask God who gives to all men generously and without reproaching, and it will be given him" (James 1:5). Jesus said, "For every one who asks receives. . ." (Matt. 7:8). There is no limit to the power of prayer. "Your Father knows what you need before you ask him" (Matt. 6:8). Why ask, then? "Because asking is something different from giving information. God waits to be asked, before He gives the gifts that supply man's deepest needs."[8]

B. Ask in Faith.

James 1:6 instructs the pray-er to "ask in faith, with no doubting, for he who doubts is like a wave of the sea that is driven and tossed by the wind." The picture is vivid; it is that of the restless waves at sea. Up and down, sideways and forward they go. Such is the man who doubts. External conditions (and inner emotional ones) determine his faith or lack of it. He is double-minded (v. 8). He believes one minute, doesn't the next. He is unstable (v. 8). Christian asking is the reverse of James' picture. It is in faith, stable, sure, deep, and real. Faith asking is single-minded asking.

C. Ask Aright.

"You ask and do not receive, because you ask wrongly, to spend it on your passions" (James 4:3). "If I had cherished

---

[8] Chadwick, *Path of Prayer*, p. 102.

iniquity in my heart, the LORD would not have listened" (Ps. 66:18). God looks down into the real intent of the heart; he knows whether the request is for godly or selfish purposes. We know, too, even though sometimes we have covered our selfish desires with clever rationalizations. But sooner or later, if we pray honestly, the subconscious mind (the receptacle of our true motivations) will yield its actual reasons for asking.

Heart belief is required for right asking: "And without faith it is impossible to please him. For whoever would draw near to God must believe that he exists and that he rewards those who seek him." Holding a grudge can block the channels to effective petition: "And whenever you stand praying, forgive, if you have anything against any one; so that your Father also who is in heaven may forgive you your trespasses" (Mark 11:25–26). Sin, unbelief, grudges, instability, a bad conscience—all can prevent asking rightly. Right motivations are essential to Christian asking.

D. Ask Righteously.

"The rightness of the asking goes down to the rightness of the asker," says Chadwick. "The person who prays is the prayer."[9] This is why James says, "Therefore confess your sins to one another, and pray for one another, that you may be healed. The prayer of a righteous man has great power in its effects" (5:16). Cornelius was "a devout man who feared God . . . and prayed constantly" (Acts 10:2); thus it was said to him by the angel, "Your prayers and your alms have ascended as a memorial before God" (Acts 10:4). John makes this principle of the righteousness of the pray-er very clear when he says, "Beloved, if our hearts do not condemn us, we have confidence before God; and we receive from him whatever we ask, *because we keep his commandments and do what pleases him*" (1 John 3:21–22, emphasis mine).

---

[9] Ibid., p. 103.

E. Ask Earnestly.

"You will seek me and find me; when you seek me with all your heart" (Jer. 29:13). Jesus' parables about importunate praying make clear the need for fervent prayer. Sincerity and earnestness go hand in hand; there is no earnestness without sincerity. Honesty and earnestness go hand in hand; how can there be earnestness without honesty? The deeply meant prayer is the earnest prayer. Such a prayer may be short or long, given once or over a period of time. But it is earnest.

F. Ask in the Spirit.

This is what Chadwick rightly calls "energized prayer." Such prayer is "inspired, instructed, and empowered of the Holy Spirit."[10] The story of Chadwick's baptism in the Spirit and how that related to his prayer life has been told earlier in this chapter. It is enough to say here that the person who has been filled with the Holy Spirit knows vital communion with God, communion in which there is real contact with the divine. (An excellent book describing the infilling of the Spirit, along with steps for entering into the experience, is the paperback by R. A. Torrey entitled, *Baptism with the Holy Spirit*, published by Bethany House, Minneapolis.)

G. Ask in Faith.

'When ye pray, believe that ye have received, and ye shall have" (Mark 11:24). Such deep, inner knowledge is the gift of God, which he must always honor. (He would not dishonor his own gift, would he?) The gift was bestowed on those of Hebrews 11, the biblical "Hall of Faith." Verse 13 stands out especially: "These all died in faith, not having received what was promised, but having seen it and greeted it from afar. . . ." Another illustration is given in John 4:46–54. At Capernaum Jesus was confronted by an official whose son was ill. He begged Jesus to heal him: " 'Sir, come down before my child dies.' " Jesus replied, " 'Go; your son shall

---

[10] Ibid., p. 104.

HOW TO UNDERSTAND THE TEACHING OF THE BIBLE ON PRAYER

live.' *The man believed the word that Jesus spoke to him and went his way"* (emphasis mine). The boy was, of course, healed. We dare not manufacture such belief. Some have "persuaded" themselves their child would be healed, when in point of fact God had not given the "prayer of faith." Such rationalization always ends in frustration and disappointment. True faith is the gift of God; when given, hold on to it. God must always honor his own gift.

FOR DISCUSSION

(Please give scriptural justification for your answers.)
1. What do we mean when we say that the power of prayer is unlimited? In what respects?
2. Explain why prayer must be in the name of Jesus.
3. What is meant by prayer "in the Spirit"? Relate this to the baptism in the Holy Spirit.
4. Discuss the Father-child relationship in prayer.
5. What does the Bible mean when it says to pray importunately?
6. Discuss the rewards of prayer.
7. Outline Chadwick's seven biblical steps in asking.

BIBLIOGRAPHY

Bounds, E. M. *Power Through Prayer.* Chicago: Moody, n.d.
Chadwick, Samuel. *The Path of Prayer.* London: Hodder and Stoughton, 1931.

6
HOW TO PRAY FOR DIVINE HEALING

Here is a true story about a Japanese student attending Asbury Theological Seminary. It is documented by Dr. Frank Bateman Stanger, President Emeritus of the Seminary.[1]

The student had returned to the seminary on a Sunday evening after conducting a meeting, only to discover that he was suffering from severe internal bleeding. By the time he arrived at the hospital he had lost two-thirds of his blood and was of course physically exhausted. In the course of a nine-week hospital stay, he sustained three major operations, each three or four hours in length. In Japan he had had three similar operations at an earlier period in his life.

After his first major operation he did well for a week. But then extreme pain attacked him in the small intestine. A four-hour operation ensued. But that did not bring freedom from illness, and ten days later the third operation was performed. He was now on the critical list, weak, unable to eat or even to consume liquids.

At the time of each operation he experienced a spiritual crisis. At the first experience he prayed because he was concerned about "my family, my school program, my finances, and so on. But I was so selfish in my praying." He prayed at the second operation because he was afraid of

[1] George Nakajima, as told to Frank B. Stanger, "The Third Prayer," *The Herald*, April 15, 1964, p. 24.

further suffering, which had already been intense. "Ironically, the second operation was the hardest of the three." Before the third surgical experience he prayed, "Lord, forgive me. I was wrong. I was so selfish. I do not know whether I can make it this time because I am so weak. But I know one thing, I need peace. . . . Thy will be done." Immediately God gave him the peace he had requested. Anxiety vanished; he thanked God.

Awaking from the third surgery, he was possessed of peace and less pain than before. But a week passed and severe pain returned; the doctor announced that this time an all-day operation was necessary. "I prayed again, 'Thy will be done.'"

At this crucial time his pastor, Clyde Van Valin, suggested a healing service. The seminarian was readied and three men—his pastor, a layman, and his seminary president—came to the hospital to pray over him. This was scriptural: "Is any among you sick? Let him call the elders of the church, and let them pray over him . . ." (James 5:14a). The three anointed the sick student with the laying on of hands. This too was scriptural: ". . . anointing him with oil in the name of the Lord" (James 5:14b). In the course of the healing service in the hospital room, the seminary president reviewed the steps in healing. Said the sick young man: "I was really impressed by his statement that faith must have some imagination in it. He said, 'Imagine yourself healed by God and for the glory of God.' I immediately imagined myself healed by God and back in Japan witnessing to my own people." Note again the scriptural validity of this procedure: "The prayer of faith will save the sick man, and the Lord will raise him up . . .' (James 5:15a).

From the moment of that healing service the young man began to mend. "I amazed the doctors." The anticipated fourth operation was never performed. The student's appetite improved. He left the hospital, then returned to theological studies. His testimony is simple and beautiful: "I have been healed by the mercy and power of God." He adds significantly: "I have rededicated my whole life to God. . . . I love Him because He loved me and holds me in His hand.... I will carry the glad tidings of salvation to my people in Japan."

He now testifies to healing due to the prayers of God's children. "Of course, God used brilliant doctors, excellent hospital equipment and highly developed medical science." But miracle was involved, too: "My doctor told one of my friends that my case was a miracle."

Healing as a result of the direct action of God upon the human body inevitably teaches us lessons of faith. It is evident from the story above that faith was strengthened and lessons learned in the course of praying for healing. A young lady of exceptional spiritual insight said, "I will be healed when God has finished teaching me the lessons he wants me to learn from my illness." The learning of lessons is part of the fabric of divine healing.

Three years ago, while at the seaside for a holiday with my family, I made the serious mistake of carrying my small son (then three years old) on my back—for hikes and even while running. His insistence to be carried was strong and I gave way to his desires. One morning I could scarcely get out of bed and was unable to lean over to tie my shoes. Back home I suffered severe back pain and hobbled to classes and appointments. The doctor prescribed a set of exercises. In the meantime I had prayed earnestly about the healing of my back. It was clear that I could not get much work done in this condition. The Spirit of God assured me of healing. But healing did not come immediately. I had to learn the importance of physical conditioning and daily exercise. It is possible that the whole event took place at the permission of God (and nature) to teach me this simple lesson. I began to go to the college gymnasium workout room, and over a period of time and by experimentation, built myself up and learned what exercises were necessary, not only for a healthy back but for all-around fitness. The whole experience proved a godsend.

Sometimes the lesson learned is not evident. E. Stanley Jones tells of an attack of diabetes. The doctor told him he could eat only certain things. As was Dr. Jones's custom, he took his problem immediately to God. He prayed to the effect that because he was traveling, it was rather impossible to follow a strict dietary pattern, so he needed to be healed lest the diabetes hinder his ministry. Finally, he was assured of healing. It did not come all at once. He asked how he would know when he was healed; the Spirit said, "by the test tube." Sure enough, in God's own time he was healed and able to eat normally. When I heard Stanley Jones tell that story, he did not indicate any lesson learned. Perhaps he himself did not know God's purpose in the illness and subsequent healing. We do not always have insight into God's ways and reasons. It is enough that God heals in his own time.

Most seasoned Christians can think of numerous examples of divine healing. The history of Christianity is replete with cases, and today they continue to occur. A minister in Olympia, Washington, experienced healing from polio, took off his back brace, hung up his crutches, and has walked ever since. From that time he has carried on a fine healing ministry; no doubt his own dramatic cure was God's way of pushing him out into the healing ministry.

A university student, suffering from a disease of long duration, went to pray with a believer who encouraged him in his desire to seek healing. He was instantly healed.

An old lady was told she must undergo surgery. Her age made surgery awkward; so with the faith of a child she prayed with her minister. She never underwent surgery. Both the young minister and the elderly woman learned of the mercy of God.

Another minister, while sitting in his study, suffered a heart attack. He went to the hospital and was put under an oxygen tent. When the tent was finally removed, the Spirit said he would now be under "a tent of divine love" for the remainder of his hospital days. "His room became a sanctuary to which people resorted to bathe themselves in the presence of God." Recently his doctor examined him and found absolutely no trace of an attack; his healing was complete.[2] His experience made him aware of God's desire to use him.

---

[2] Frank Bateman Stanger, "Some Recent Experiences in the Field of Healing," *The Herald*, May 13, 1964, p. 24.

"If the Spirit of him who raised Jesus from the dead dwells in you, he who raised Christ Jesus from the dead will give life to your mortal bodies also through his Spirit which dwells in you" (Rom. 8:11).

I. THE STEPS IN DIVINE HEALING.

In the story of the Japanese student, the young man referred to the steps in healing as shared with him by President Stanger of Asbury Seminary. Dr. Stanger published these in *The Herald* for October 2, 1963:

A. Relax.

The first step to healing is relaxation. The body is "forgotten" in order to permit the mind to center upon God and his great power.

B. Be Cleansed.

The second step is cleansing. The whole person, including the conscious and subconscious mind, must be purified so that God's healing power can course through the seeker.

C. Seek Clarification of God's Will.

The third step is simply asking God what *precisely* is needed for healing to occur. In response, God will make his will clear.

D. Expect Healing.

This means actually believing God has heard the prayer and will answer it. The posture is active faith; half faith will not do.

E. Relinquish Yourself.

The fifth step is the giving of one's life, without reservation, into God's hands. In this phase of prayer, the seeker's recaptured health is given over to God for *his* holy purposes, for *his* glory, for *his* kingdom.

F. Begin Living the Promise.

In this final step, the pray-er extends his hands to receive the promised gift. He commences to live and act in the strength of the health-giving power received. There is nothing left now but to thank God.

II. SPIRITUAL HEALING.

Notice that early in Dr. Stanger's list of steps to healing is spiritual cleansing. It is no accident that Jesus said to the paralytic who had been let down through the roof, "Man, your sins are forgiven you" (Luke 5:20). It is significant that Jesus forgave his sins before healing his body. Spiritual healing or cleansing frequently comes before physical healing. The removal of guilt makes way for the acceptance of healing. Karl Menninger says, "Guilt changes the physical structure of the body and makes the person more susceptible to disease."

Counselors know there is an interrelation between spiritual, emotional, and physical dimensions of the person. A young homemaker suffered from ill health so severely she had not had a full night's sleep in nine years. She heard and believed the Good News of full salvation, prayed for forgiveness and spiritual renewal, and received both. The next morning she awoke to realize she had slept through the night uninterrupted. "Could it be that I am healed?" she asked herself. (Interestingly enough, she had not prayed for physical healing, only for spiritual cleansing.) She hardly dared believe physical restoration had come. But the next night's rest was also uninterrupted, and the next, and the next. She had in fact been cured of a disease that had awakened her nightly for nine years! Her spirit had been cleansed by the power of God; one result was physical healing.

Modern psychiatric medicine is making increasingly clear the relation of the interior and exterior dimensions of man. If the interior is colored by guilt or disruption, the result can be poor health. Inner cleanness is related to good health, physical and mental. Recall again Menninger's statement: "Guilt changes the physical structure of the body and makes the person more susceptible to disease." The same thing is said in the Bible in this language: ". . . The prayer of faith will save the sick man, and the Lord will raise him up; and if he has committed sins, he will be forgiven. Therefore confess your sins to one another, and pray for one another, that you may be healed. The prayer of a righteous man has great power in its effects" (James 5:15–16).

III. MENTAL SUGGESTION.

Here we are particularly interested in the role of suggestion (and auto-suggestion) in the healing process. First, we come upstanding to a law of human nature: Psychological influences can cause illness; by the same token they can cure it. The story is told of college students who tricked Ernie (not his real name) into believing he was ill. He came to classes feeling normal. His classmates, one by one and independently, commented upon his sickly appearance. By noon he was home in bed, actually feeling ill.

Some do not need to have a trick like that played on them to make them ill. They have made themselves ill, for they have played the trick on themselves. They have developed the habit of expecting illness. Some people want to be ill; it is a device for obtaining something. The true story is told of an aunt who always arrived ill at the annual family reunion. Relatives scurried around giving her aid. But when it came time to eat, she consumed as big a share as anyone. Apparently she was ill to get attention. Incidentally, it will do no good to pray for healing if one does not really *want* it. It would not be surprising to learn that the aunt had prayed repeatedly for health—but that would not have been true prayer. She must want normality more than attention; to put it another way, she must learn natural ways of acceptance. Requests of God must be characterized by utter sincerity, even desperation.

What percentage of human illnesses are caused by

psychological influences no one really knows. But we can take Dr. Blaine E. McLaughlin's statements as reflective of current thinking. He is director of psychiatry at Women's Medical College, Philadelphia. He declares that 60 to 85 percent of the people who come to doctor's offices suffer from psychosomatic problems. Ninety-nine percent of headaches, he says, are psychologically caused, as are 75 percent of gastric problems, 75 percent of skin disorders, 85 percent of asthmatic conditions. Said a heart specialist—to quote another physician's opinion—85 percent of heart cases reveal nothing structurally wrong; it is fear that causes the disturbance. Now this is not to say that people suffering from psychological influences are not truly ill; they are. And the tragic truth of the matter is that they don't need to be! They have yielded to negative mental suggestion.

Even the healing of broken bones can be retarded (or halted) by negative, pessimistic thinking. The "power of positive thinking" is not all nonsense, as some would try to make out; there is great truth in it. Its danger is in thinking that all problems can be solved by this method. It is not a substitute for God's supernatural invasion of our lives; it is rather a natural process assisting and working with the supernatural process. It is a well-known fact that when apathy or helplessness is driven out and hope reinstated, chances for recovery are much higher. One authority says that 80 percent of all known diseases benefit materially by positive suggestion.

Wholesome thinking not only assists in the healing process, it also aids in the maintenance of good health. Here are eight suggestions for healthful thinking:

A. Look Outward.

Instead of continuous and habitual self-analysis ("I wonder if I'm going to be well today"), expect the best and let the dominant thrust of your thinking be outside yourself. Think about the beauty of God's world, the planned activities of the day (with its challenges), and especially the needs of others. The Reverend E. E. Helms, a man born with a poor body, forced to use crutches on occasion and no stranger to pain, lived to be very old (and always helpful) because he disciplined himself to think of things outside of, and people other than, himself.

B. Enjoy Life.

You can find many reasons for enjoying your way of life. Your work has its many fine aspects, even if it is not that ideal job you longed for in youth. It has its challenges and fringe benefits. It has its elements of joy. So it is with all phases of your life. Put yourself in the frame of mind that sees the joyful and minimizes the doleful.

C. Find a Hobby.

At a recent psychological society meeting, it was stated by a therapist that he had not known of a single person institutionalized for mental breakdown who had had an absorbing hobby. It appears that distraction from the routine of life and work is material to good mental health . . . and if to mental health, then to physical well-being.

D. Have a Good Attitude About People.

Do not let yourself drift into the indoor sport called "gossip." Some people are constantly running others down (feeble attempts at blowing up one's own balloon). This is tragic and detrimental. Never hold a grudge; never afford yourself the luxury of "getting even" (even in socially acceptable ways). If someone has done you harm, act as if it had not happened (rarely does one need to "clear it up" through personal encounter). In all probability it will "blow over" sooner or later; in the meantime you have saved yourself psychological anguish, and probably physical anguish, too.

E. Accept Your Circumstances.

Then learn to live with what cannot be changed. Dr. Ida Scudder's father wisely told her in her youth not to allow herself to be upset by what could not be changed. Get on with what can be changed, he counseled.

F. Learn to Endure Adversity.

Paul, writing from prison (!) said, "I know how to be abased, and I know how to abound; in any and all circumstances I have learned the secret of facing plenty and hunger, abundance and want. I can do all things in him who strengthens me" (Phil. 4:12-13). He did not let adverse circumstances fester.

G. Find a Reason to Laugh.

Whatever the circumstances, be cheerful if not downright humorous. E. Stanley Jones recommends looking into the mirror to practice smiling and laughing. He says that sometimes we should burst out laughing for no reason at all. There is something therapeutic in laughter. It is the gift of God.

H. Make Clear Decisions.

Finally, learn that making a decision is often the best tranquilizer. Indecision is related to mental illness. Executives and administrators have had to learn to make decisions, even at the risk of making mistakes. They have had to learn the further lesson of letting the decision rest once it is made. None must allow himself to say over and again, "Should I do this or that?" or "Have I made a mistake?" Repeated again and again to the point of abnormality, this sort of agonizing is tragic in its consequences. Make your decision and leave it there.

The Christian view of positive thinking—of wholesome mental suggestion—is summed up by Paul from prison: "...Whatever is true, whatever is honorable, whatever is just, whatever is pure, whatever is lovely, whatever is gracious, if there is any excellence, if there is anything worthy of praise, think about these things" (Phil. 4:8).

IV. MEDICAL SCIENCE.

Medicine and surgery are God's gifts to the world. As gifts they are to be received with gratitude. This was obviously Paul's position, because Luke accompanied him as his private physician.

Medical checkups, including periodic chest X-rays, constitute Christian duties. Carelessness can cause illness and death, making work and heartache (and financial reverse) for loved ones. Also included in our Christian obligations are enough sleep, exercise, relaxation and recreation (including restorative vacation periods), proper eating habits (how many die prematurely due to being overweight!), and eliminating harmful personal habits. Christians must take a serious look at smoking and drinking. The Surgeon General's staff has found on several occasions that smoking is a cause of cancer; those reports must be taken seriously if we really believe that our bodies are the temples of the living God. Medical science has demonstrated that smokers and drinkers are more susceptible to all diseases.

John Wesley, though no physician, gave this simple prescription for good health; it includes helpful spiritual advice:

> Observe . . . exactness in your regimen or manner of living. Use plain diet. Go to bed early. Above all, add . . . that old unfashionable medicine, prayer. Be as clean and sweet as possible in houses, clothes, and furniture. Water is the wholesomest of all drinks; quickens the appetite, and strengthens the digestion most. Spiritous liquors are a certain, though slow, poison. Exercise is indispensably necessary to health and long life. Walking is the best exercise. All violent and sudden passions dispose to . . . acute diseases. The love of God . . . prevents all the bodily disorders the passions introduce, by keeping the passions themselves within due bounds.[3]

---

[3] *Journal*, June 11, 1747.

V. DIET.

Improper eating patterns constitute a major problem in today's society. A young diabetic, knowing full well the seriousness of his condition, refuses to control his diet; the result is frequent stays in the hospital. A young lady with high ideals and noble life goals finds herself continually frustrated by overweight; having lost respect for herself, she finds that few others respect her. Overeating is frequently due to emotional reasons. It takes self-discipline to follow the line of moderation; the line of least resistance is sure to lead to health problems, both mental and physical.

Even as uncontrolled eating can cause poor health, so scientifically disciplined eating can aid in bringing about good health. Every clinic today has mimeographed diet sheets for people whose medical problems fall into well-defined categories. It is important that diet programs be followed under doctor's orders; homemade programs can be dangerous. The balanced diet is common knowledge, and today vitamin supplements can be used when necessary.

It does little good to pray for health if we are following unhealthful eating practices. Prayer is always cooperative—God and man working together.

VI. HEALING THROUGH INVOLVEMENT.

Something rejuvenative happens to people when they feel truly needed and as a result involve themselves in a meaningful task. John Wesley suffered from tuberculosis; on one occasion he bled internally so profusely that he was forced to strip and jump into an icy stream to halt the flow of blood. Outdoor preaching, horseback riding, the sense of being needed in a great evangelistic task, divine providence—these combined to sustain his health through many years of fruitful service.

Remember the experience of Glen Cunningham who, badly burned, nevertheless became the fastest runner of his generation. Determination, hard work, and involvement in running competition did the trick.

Don Zimmerman had polio. His determination to get

HOW ARE YOU PRAYING?

well, plus his involvement in a consistent walking and exercise program, returned him to normality. Today he is a normal man engaged in military chaplaincy. In telling his story, he says the exercises "hurt"; but that did not stop him.

Don Wilson also contracted polio. His physician said he would never have a normal life. Don said it would be otherwise. He took his first painful steps and finally learned to walk again. He dared to go water skiing, then skied every Saturday, developing the strength of his leg muscles. He graduated from dental school and today is a dentist highly respected in his community. Physical exercise, involvement in a challenging academic and professional program—these have helped to restore his health.

While I was a tennis coach, one of the boys who joined my team had been badly burned. His hands and face appeared irreparable (though he has since received much help from a plastic surgeon). I admired his stoical determination to become a first-rate tennis player. His right thumb was stunted and badly scarred, the skin below it tender. Often he finished a match with bleeding hands, the skin having broken under the strain of gripping and swinging the racket. But he completed the year as one of our better players.

Toyohiko Kagawa, perhaps the most effective of Japan's modern evangelists, was told he would die before reaching middle age. Instead he lived past seventy. His doctor told him on one occasion that he must go to the country for sunshine and fresh air if he wished to live half a year longer; instead Kagawa went to the slums of Kobe and, as someone put it, he "forgot to die." He saw the slums cleared, needy people aided, and souls won into the kingdom of God. The excitement and challenge of his ministry led to his own improved health. Involvement in Christian service saved his life.

Involvement does not always bring about the complete restoration of health. It did not for Kagawa. Nor did it for Jack Arnold, an insurance agent in the city of Seattle who suffers from muscular dystrophy. But Mr. Arnold is more active than most in community and church affairs. When his legs ache, he goes to the office where, he confesses, "Involvement steers my thinking away from my pain. It helps to go to work." There is a sense in which he experiences daily healing because he gives himself to daily involvement. And he believes it is the grace of God that gives him strength and sufficient health for each day. He runs a thriving business and has a family of five children.

VII. JESUS AND HEALING.

There can be no question that Jesus is a healer; indeed, one of his biblical names is *Healer*. He regarded healing as integral to his ministry; a passage like Matthew 9:18-34 makes that clear: A woman touched the hem of his garment and was healed of a twelve-year hemorrhage; a ruler's dead daughter was brought back to life; two blind men were made to see; a dumb demoniac was cured. Yes, Christ was a healer. Moreover, he commissioned his apostles to heal, and a reading of the Gospels and Acts makes clear that they did heal. The apostle Paul also healed, and he distinguished healing as a gift of the church (1 Cor. 12, 14). Throughout church history there have been witnesses to the continuing power of Christ, through his Spirit, to heal the body. The healing ministry of Christ and of his present-day apostles continues.

In the Bible disease is sometimes associated with Satan. Said Jesus, "And ought not this woman, a daughter of Abraham whom Satan bound for eighteen years, be loosed from this bond on the sabbath day?" (Luke 13:16). Acts 10:38 says Jesus "went about doing good and healing all that were oppressed by the devil, for God was with him." Though some illness is traced to Satan, Jesus was angry with those who said it was necessarily due to personal sin: " 'Rabbi, who sinned, this man or his parents, that he was born blind?' Jesus replied, 'It was not that this man sinned, or his parents, but that the works of God might be made manifest in him' " (John 9:2-3).

The Bible includes healing in the plan of redemption. In the classic prophetic passage on our Lord's earthly mission in Isaiah 53, we read, "Surely he has borne our griefs and carried our sorrows" (v. 4a). The same chapter says that "with his stripes we are healed" (v. 5). In Matthew 8 we see this prophecy fulfilled: "That evening they brought to him many who were possessed with demons; and he cast out the spirits with a word, and healed all that were sick." This was to fulfill what was spoken by the prophet Isaiah, "He took our infirmities and bore our diseases" (vv. 16–17). Samuel Chadwick observed that this cannot mean that illnesses "were transferred to Him, for, so far as we know, He was never sick, but in sympathy and at great cost in physical and mental virtue He lifted their burden and bore it away."[4]

But while provision is made through the power of Christ to heal our bodies, not all illnesses are in fact removed. Why? Some illness is the gift of God, given for a specific and noble purpose. Was Job's illness of grace? Some say so. This much we know: It proved to be to the glory of God. And Paul's? He prayed more than once for the removal of his illness, which he called a "thorn in the flesh," yet God did not see fit to remove it. Paul tells us why: "And to keep me from being too elated by the abundance of revelations, a thorn was given me in the flesh, a messenger of Satan, to harass me, to keep me from being too elated" (2 Cor. 12:7; cf. Gal. 4:13). It is significant that Paul had the gift of healing and many were cured at the touch of his hands; but Paul, like Christ, accepted his own sufferings. The fact is that some are healed, such as Epaphroditus (Phil. 2:27) and some are not, such as Trophimus (2 Tim. 4:20). Was there some lesson to be taught Trophimus? Was there to be some benefit to others? Frequently answers to those questions are not to be found; they are bathed in mystery. It is good enough to say, Let the will of the Lord be done.

Some illnesses are the natural product of disobeying God's laws through overeating, bad personal habits, carelessness, and such. Other illnesses are apparently the more direct product of grace. "I am bound," said Chadwick, "to believe that sickness may be in the will of God, for the purpose of discipline, for the glory of His grace, and the Ministry of Christ."[5]

But having said that, it is necessary to know that many

---

[4]Samuel Chadwick, *The Path of Prayer* (London: Hodder and Stoughton, 1931), p. 119.
[5]Ibid., p. 120.

HOW TO PRAY FOR DIVINE HEALING

are sick who do not need to be. If sin or guilt feelings are the cause, let them be removed through forgiveness to make way for release and bodily health. If the obstacle to faith has not been discovered, let the Scriptures be searched and earnest prayer made for divine insight. Also, let it be known that the most life-giving, health-giving existence is the joyful life in Christ. The healthiest, happiest life is the Christian life. That is a simple fact known by those who live an obedient life of faith.

Suppose, however, that you live the obedient life of faith and still find no healing. What should be your attitude in this situation?

First, it will do no good to berate yourself. The illness has come through no fault of your own; leave it at that.

Second, it will do no good to accuse God. Trust that he knows what he is doing.

Third, remember that some illnesses will not be healed until the resurrection, when wholeness and a fullness of life hitherto unknown will be the gifts of every Christian (1 Cor. 15:35ff.).

FOR DISCUSSION

1. Do you believe in the fact of divine healing? Back up your answer with (a) Scripture and (b) an illustration from your own life or an acquaintance.
2. Review the steps to healing under Heading I.
3. Discuss Karl Menninger's statement about guilt and disease. What part does forgiveness play in healing?
4. Discuss healing as related to mental suggestion. Review the eight suggestions for positive, healthy thinking.
5. Discuss the role of medical science in maintaining good health. What about smoking and drinking?
6. What is the role of proper eating as related to good health?
7. What is meant by healing through involvement? Give some illustrations, either from the text or your own observation.
8. How did Jesus view healing? How does the prophecy of Isaiah 53 fit into the picture? Do you agree with Chadwick that some "sickness may be in the will of God"? Give your own reasons why being a Christian is the healthiest way to live. If one is a Christian and still not healed what should be that person's attitude?

BIBLIOGRAPHY

Chadwick, Samuel. *The Path of Prayer*. London: Hodder and Stoughton, 1931.

Jones, E. Stanley. *Abundant Living*. New York: Abingdon, 1942.

———. *The Word Became Flesh*. New York: Abingdon, 1963.

Marshall, Catherine (LeSourd). *Beyond Our Selves*. New York: McGraw-Hill, 1961.

7

HOW TO PRAY WITH YOUR FAMILY

In this chapter we will seek to see the dynamics as well as the methods of family prayer. We must understand and develop those family relationships that make prayer possible. Family prayer does not take place in a vacuum; it flows out of a way of family living; indeed, it is a way of living. So it is that husbands and wives pray together if they are happy and compatible. Parents and children commune with God best when their relationships are normal. Young adults leave home to be useful citizens and praying people when they have been brought up under the tutelage of parents who are righteous, praying Christians.

I. HUSBANDS AND WIVES.[1]

Christian couples will have prayer experiences together before marriage. At the wedding, the marriage will be sealed by the prayers of the minister. And from the first day they set up housekeeping, they will have worship in their home. Starting on that footing will assist greatly in the development and maintenance of a truly Christian home.

Now this growing prayer fellowship between husband and wife emerges with difficulty if their compatibility is

---

[1] In this section I am indebted to E. Stanley Jones, *Abundant Living*, pp. 272-73 for helpful and motivating suggestions.

marred. To put it positively, the greater the compatibility—provided it reflects adjustment around Jesus Christ—the stronger the life in Christ, and therefore the stronger the prayer life. Below are some ground rules for the husband-and-wife relationship that are conducive to a better spiritual life in marriage. Bear in mind, as all of them are spelled out, that they suggest not only a way of compatibility, but a way of prayer—for, to repeat, prayer is a relationship and a rich experience out of which actual verbal prayer can flow the more easily.

A. Ground Rules for Husband and Wife.

1. *Resist the temptation to pick at each other.* A free, joyous, happy way of domestic happiness cannot be attained if one party nags. Incidentally, that is a good rule to remember in rearing children; to nag at them continuously has its damaging results both in the present and the future.

2. *Accept your partner for what he or she is.* To attempt to remake your partner will not do. (I once saw a farmer "remade" into a city man by his wife. He was the most uncomfortable man on earth!) See the God-given characteristics in your sweetheart. Concentrate on these, not upon the limitations.

3. *Avoid comparing your partner with someone else supposedly better.* In the novel *Nicholas Nickleby,* Charles Dickens has Mantalini say to his wife that he is a fine husband " 'who might have married two countesses and a dowager.'

" 'Two countesses,' interposed Madame. 'You told me one before.'

" 'Two!' cried Mantalini. 'Two . . . fine women, real countesses and splendid fortunes. . . .' "

Mantalini and his wife had had words; in trying to justify himself he attempted to reflect upon his wife—his technique being to compare her unfavorably with other women, others he supposedly could have married. They were countesses and they had fortunes! How much better either of them than his present wife, is the implication. Naturally Mrs. Mantalini asks him why, if they were so great, he didn't marry one of them. He then tries to say something nice to make his wife feel better.

This passage is intended as humor. But when it happens in real life it is seldom humorous!

4. *Show your love in little ways.* Flowers for the wife, a favorite dish for the husband, little comments of appreciation by both—these are the kinds of things that keep a marriage relationship alive. Somehow it is not sufficient to earn a handsome salary or to own a nice car and a fashionable home. These things are of course good; but the little things have their place, too, and as it turns out they hold the enduring place. We all need to be reminded that we are appreciated and needed, and for happily married couples these expressions of acceptance are couched in the language and deeds of true love.

5. *Learn that the highest and best form of sexual experience is truly spiritual.* This God-given urge is not to be squelched; rather, the sexual relationship teaches us something very deep and real about the beautiful side of life, and therefore about the spiritual. Selfish expression blocks spiritual impression.

Break any one of these five rules and see how difficult it is to pray together. When a rule is broken, be quick to make amends and see how readily your capacity to pray returns. The same principle holds true with reference to the following ten ground rules for husbands.

B. Ground Rules for the Husband.

1. *Remember to remember.* Your wedding anniversary, your wife's birthday, Mother's Day, and other special occasions are very meaningful to her and, when celebrated within their proper Christian context, carry their own spiritual significance. Remember to take her out to dinner on occasion for no reason at all. The love relationship must be developed and maintained just like any other relationship in life. How many couples fall away from each other because they forget to continue to "court" after marriage!

2. *Never criticize your wife in the presence of others.* This is

extremely embarrassing, and the principle is sufficiently self-explanatory that it needs no further comment here.

3. *Your wife must have a voice in the management of the money.* Not only for herself (which is very important since she must maintain her own identity and independence), but for the family as well. Some studies show that more domestic problems and divorces occur over money than any other single factor. And don't forget that giving to God's work is a form of praise and therefore of prayer. Share that experience with your wife.

4. *When you come home at night, bring into the home an air of gaiety and strength.* Fathers lend to the home a certain character if they are full of faith and strength. Your wife may be weary, moody, suffering from the cloistered feeling that comes with keeping the children all day. Here is your chance to give her a much-needed lift. Breathe a prayer as you enter the home that you will be God's messenger of inspiration.

5. *Plan your recreation and vacation experiences together.* Fishing and hunting are great! But many women do not enjoy them. Nor is this to say the man of the house has no right to his own occasional recreation experiences. But a good chunk of your leisure time should be devoted to doing things together or with the whole family. Your wife needs your fellowship, guidance, and strength in these out-of-the-house activities.

6. Along the same line, *prepare to listen.* When your wife wants to talk, give a listening ear just to her. She wants to share with the most important person in her life what she has been doing, her latest ideas in clothing or home decoration, her new enthusiasms on any subject. *Listening* is the key word here.

7. *Frequently tell your wife she is the greatest woman in the world.* Showing your admiration for her skills (such as cooking, sewing, child rearing) will make this concrete. But don't forget to tell her point-blank that she is the greatest. A husband truly in love believes that.

8. *Worship together.* In the home read the Scriptures aloud, verbalize prayers, share personal insights from your own reading and meditation. Encourage your wife to do the same. Attend public worship services together, too. In

corporate worship there is a kind of strength for the whole family. The couple that worships together stays together.

9. *Have an eye only for your wife.* The man who "suddenly" runs off with another woman surely hasn't changed all that suddenly. There was a first glance, a permitted thought, a mounting of desire, an entertaining of sinful thoughts—then it happened! Reserve your thoughts and heart only for her.

10. *Cherish your wife ". . . in sickness and in health."* The vow made at the marriage altar must be remembered. Make a patient, consistent effort to understand her in all her ways and moods. Help her achieve her goals, her sense of fulfillment. Help her through times of moodiness, weariness, illness.

C. Ground Rules for the Wife.

1. *Learn that the chief source of your strength is in God.* Your daily devotional experiences are the most important help available to you. In his strength you can meet the little irritations and disappointments with assurance. And in turn, what a strength you will be to your husband. There is nothing so discouraging as a defeated wife.

2. *Work along with your husband in making home worship regular.* Frankly, some wives have to take the initiative in grace before meals and family worship. But once the habit is established, it enlists the cooperation of both husband and wife. Mom can remind Dad to read from the Bible before the children run off to school or play. And you can initiate family worship in many other ways. E. Stanley Jones makes a most interesting suggestion: Create a "shrine in the home where your husband, you, or your children can retire and be undisturbed for quiet meditation and prayer."[2]

3. *Be actively engaged in the life and work of the church.* Once again, the wife may have to nudge the husband into the church. It is obvious she cannot do this if she herself is not so involved. Every mature Christian should have at least one

---
[2] Ibid., p. 273.

regular job in the church—Sunday school teacher, organist, youth fellowship advisor, or something else. This kind of involvement, when entered into wholeheartedly, pays off in high returns.

(Of course, there is the wife who spends so much time in church activities that she forgets her husband and children! This kind of involvement pays off, too, . . . in the tragic loss of her family.)

4. *Be intelligently interested in your husband's work.* Even as he must listen to you, so you must listen to him. His work is in a sense his life (especially if he is in one of the professions such as teaching, medicine, law, or the ministry). He needs your help and advice; especially he needs your loving understanding about his problems and goals. Your alert interest is absolutely imperative to him. Many a woman has lost her husband due to disinterest in his work.

5. *Have a heart when it comes to finance!* Don't spend your husband's money faster than he makes it. Indeed, don't spend it faster than makes him comfortable. Even as you must have your own spending money and share in the family budget, so you must avoid the temptation of "grabbing" what he has brought home. Let him play his rightful role of authority in this as well as other matters. And in the last analysis, happy financial relationships come out of cooperative effort.

6. *Be a part of your husband's family.* When you married him, you married into a family. Respect the members of it. Show attention to his mother especially.

7. *Don't hold out for something that doesn't make that much difference.* Lots of husband-and-wife arguing is merely ego expression. To win the argument is the whole point. But why argue over things that don't count? Give in, rather than win and made a rift.

8. *Practice humility.* If you always have the right answer, you are not wise. Part of the charm of true femininity is subtlety—that ability to make him think he is right. That takes a certain humility, of course. But the know-it-all does not make a good wife.

9. *Dress to make him comfortable.* Your community, and his work if he is a professional man, are the determining factors.

Discover that level, equip your wardrobe accordingly. If he feels at ease with you in public, this will be of great benefit to him.

10. *Make your house into a home.* You are rightfully called a homemaker in our society. That is your province. It is a noble province. It is perhaps the greatest of all callings. The pictures you hang on the walls, the kind of interior decorations you suggest, the way you prepare the meals, and all the other things that go into creative domesticity—these create the thing we call home atmosphere. If you have established the atmosphere suggested by the image of the crackling fire, the smell of cooking when he comes home at night, the children playing on the floor, you are making a happy husband.

D. The Prayer Application.

In advance of listing the ground rules, it was stated that (1) keeping the rules was important to make prayer possible. That is to say, prayer flows out of a normal, compatible Christian marriage. At least the potential for prayer originates there. (2) By the same token, breaking the ground rules will raise a barrier that makes prayer difficult if not impossible.

Now to these two observations we add a third: Because you are human, areas of weakness will come to your attention as you read through the rules. Make these weaknesses special objects of prayer. Attack them in the power of God, for the making of a happier and more Christian marriage.

II. ESPECIALLY FOR PARENTS OF PRESCHOOL CHILDREN.

Over a century ago, Horace Bushnell could say, "Let every mother and father realize that when their child is three years of age, they have done more than half they will ever do for its character." Plato said, "The most important part of education is right training in the nursery." In our own day, Ernest Ligon echoes the same truth in this statement, "I think it can be said conservatively that a college student in his four years does not make proportionately a fraction of the progress that a well-trained infant does in his first two years." Jenkins, Shacter, and Bauer, in *These Are Your Children*, say, "Probably at no period of life does a child accomplish as much as during the pre-school years." So whether we are thinking of the development of character, the establishing of attitudes (religious or otherwise), or laying a foundation for more mature learning, the preschool years are extremely important.

The first two and a half or three years of a child's life are the most important for establishing right attitudes toward God and prayer to him.

A. Learning About God Begins at Birth.

Psychologists tell us that a baby begins to learn as soon as the "five" senses are opened. The senses are the channels through which experience enters the tiny personality; they are the vehicles by which experience writes its impressions on the mind. Coupled with the sensory apparatus is the indispensable and undefinable dimension of mother love. Somehow a child begins to know whether he is wanted or not, even on the first day of his life. If mother really wants her baby, the infant begins to feel secure and with the passing days he soon senses that he "belongs."

Now this feeling of security has a direct bearing on the kind of God which is emerging in the child's mind. This is the principle at work: If the child sees in his parent a kind, loving, dependable person, in all probability his earliest concept of God is kind, loving, and one in whom he can place trust. The amazing fact is that parents, by their very character, tend to determine and formulate their child's idea of God. The point to underscore here is that on the very first day of his life—even from the moment mother first takes the infant in her arms—the formulation of a concept of God begins. It is a tiny beginning to be sure, but the significance of that beginning cannot be overestimated. This developing concept of God will shape greatly the real character of his later prayer experiences.

B. Family Worship With Small Children.

The atmosphere of the home is of primary importance for the development of a successful devotional attitude in our children. If the atmosphere communicates God and love for him, the child absorbs and catches that. If it is otherwise (neutrality toward God and prayer, or outright antagonism), the child quickly absorbs that. True devotion is established in the soul of a child by observing and experiencing the normal round of activities as well as the more formal religious practices of the home, because in the truly Christian home everything thought, said, and done reflects a righteous way of life.

In other words, the sum total of things, activities, and parental attitudes combine to mold the child. And this molding process begins the very first day the baby is home from the hospital. This is why devotion to Christ cannot wait until some "later day"; it is imperative that it be firmly established by the time of marriage if we want our children to catch that religious devotion. What one's home is, the child is becoming. That is common knowledge, and it is at once beautiful and terrible in its implications. What responsibility for parents! A God-serving home makes devout children. Of course we see exceptions, but this is the rule.

As to the more formal religious practices, the obvious place to begin is grace before meals. We do not say, "The baby cannot know what is going on; therefore, we will not pray before meals." The baby does know! We say grace habitually and always. And when he is old enough to talk, how refreshing to hear his own spontaneous prayers! Memorized graces are good in their place (every family should know and use them occasionally), but the simple, heartfelt "thank you" of a child undeniably brings the whole family closer to God and themselves.

Praying over the cradle, then later kneeling beside the bed—these devotional acts do not go unheeded. The child is absorbing all this, and one day he himself will pray a simple prayer. Bedtime prayers develop through the years; all the while a solid foundation of devotion in family members is being constructed.

Bible reading and family singing also have their place as praises, prayers, and devotions. As soon as possible give the child his own Bible (say at age three); the sense of possession is the beginning of a healthy respect for "God's Book." Obviously he will not be able to read it very soon, but the Book is *his own*. The sense of possession is very important to the small child, as to the older. Mother or father may paraphrase an appropriate story from the Bible or read from a Bible storybook. Not till the child is a good deal older should there be much longer reading. Stories from the Gospels and selected portions of the Old Testament (e.g., 1 Samuel) are the best for telling to children. Short prayers after Bible reading (two or three sentences at first) are recommended; even better, let the child himself pray as early as he can. This he loves to do.

Christian singing is praise, a form of prayer. There are now available more fine hymnbooks for family and children than ever. Some of them are beautifully graded. But why not begin by singing together a grace before meals? Perhaps you will want to use one with the richness of family tradition from your own childhood, or one in German or French. And as to a hymnbook, families have found that to make their own is an opportunity for creativity and doing something together. Procedure is simple: Secure a five-by-seven looseleaf notebook. On a righthand page paste a children's hymn (cut out of a Sunday school take-home sheet, for example); on the lefthand page attach a colorful picture (say from a magazine) which complements the story of the song opposite. The book does not have to be completed in one sitting (the child's attention span will not be that long anyway); add to it as the children bring home new songs from Sunday school.

Whatever the format for family prayers, let them be habitual. Right after breakfast is perhaps the best time; or if father is away at work before the family is up, then in the evening when everyone can be together.

III. WORSHIP AND THE DEVELOPING FAMILY.

In their preadolescent years, children are followers. Take advantage of this characteristic and lead them into regular, habitual devotional paths. Family worship must be habitual, as reflected in the custom of praying before bedtime or attending Sunday school and public worship. Christian families just do these things; they do not leave the door open to debate. That kind of casual attitude toward God is quickly perceived by our children, and later in life (if not now!) they try to force us to make other exceptions. The worship of God does not have exceptions. It is like taking our meals; it is just done. To be sure, there is variety in the ways we worship him (e.g., on family vacation when as a family we create our own worship service). But the point is clear that we always take time at appropriate times to worship God.

Your own private devotional life has a powerful influence upon your children. Sooner or later they observe your habits. They soon learn of your love for the Bible, God, and righteousness. They know your view of Jesus and his Cross. All these things are quickly sensed and poured into the developing personalities of your children.

When the adolescent period sets in (realize that the age at which this occurs will vary with individual children), your children may no longer have a tendency to follow your pattern. They are terribly anxious to adopt the pattern of their peers; but in the family, the situation may be quite different. Here we must be patient and rely upon the solid foundation built into our children from infancy. The chances are that family worship, along with worship and Bible learning experiences in the church, are making an impression upon their lives after all. In fact, there may be a new kind of sensitivity, a new flowering of our children's spirituality in adolescence; some authorities tell us that adolescence is a very important time for the development of religious experience. Youth at this age often make religious decisions. Many people are converted at this age, though the ideal age is much earlier. We must remind ourselves that the adolescent is self-conscious, many times awkward, and is finding his way. But through all this, God is seeking him out through nature, learning, and in the devotional experiences of his home, which, after all, is still his real security.

If you can arrange to send your children to a Christian college in an evangelical tradition, they will have their devotional habits strengthened and deepened. That may be true in a public university, too, especially if they have the chance to affiliate with Inter-Varsity Christian Fellowship or a similar group. But this much must be underscored: *The college years are extremely important in shaping a young person's philosophy of life.* That development should include some advancement in the practice and appreciation of prayer and God's Word. One significant advantage of the Christian college is its offering of Bible classes, for which regular credit is given, and which are taught by evangelical scholars whose dual aim is the development of character and the communication of the Word of God. The informal Bible study and prayer groups add to the value of the college experience.

When young people go out into the world of business and the professions, they will in all probability follow in the footsteps of their parents. If parents have been devout and contributive citizens, their children will be the same. But some children leave home for the work-a-day world without Christ. This is a most heartbreaking experience for serious Christian parents. It is important that parents not berate themselves; any of us could have done better at child rearing. But if disappointments come, let us hang onto God in earnest prayer. *The most important thing we ever do for our children, whatever their ages, is to pray for them.* The fervent prayer is honored, says God's Word.

And we have explicit prayer promises for our children. One of the best of these is Acts 2:39, where Peter says, "For the promise is to you and to your children and to all that are far off, every one whom the Lord our God calls to him." You may also want to invite close friends to join you in prayer for your unsaved children. No one will want to talk to very many, and it will surely do no good to impress yourself and others negatively until faith itself is worn threadbare. But to have a prayer partner or two for something as serious as this will bring comfort and genuine help. And when you see your children, live with the air of Christian expectancy. Let your faith show. Trust that the seed of the Gospel has been sown and that salvation will come in God's own time. Let the principle of faith operate; be released to it always and forever. This deep faith has its telling result.

FOR DISCUSSION

1. Which of the ground rules did you find particularly relevant to your own marriage? Will you make weaknesses a special object of prayer with a view, not to berating yourself, but to changing?
2. Why are the preschool years so important? What basic attitudes are established? You may find it helpful in discussion to take Ernest Ligon's statement as the kick-off point.
3. Discuss family worship as you practice it at your house. Indicate the ages of your children and how you make prayer meaningful or interesting.
4. If you have no children, how do you and your spouse have worship?
5. Do you agree that your own private devotional life has a bearing on your child's developing attitude toward God and prayer? Explain.

BIBLIOGRAPHY

Jenkins, Gladys Gardner; Helen Shacter; William W. Bauer, M.D. *These Are Your Children.* New York: Scott, Foresman, 1953.

Jones, E. Stanley. *Abundant Living.* New York: Abingdon, 1942.

Trent, Robbie. *Your Child and God.* New York: Macmillan.

8

HOW TO FACE THE CHALLENGES OF PRAYER

We are so constructed that life must have challenge. In our sports, obstacles are created: the golf course has its mounds, the track field its length, the tennis court its net. These man-imposed obstacles make the games interesting. The obstacles in prayer are not imposed, they are just there. They are often frustrating if not exasperating. But it is in this very business of coping with difficulty in the presence of God that some of our finest development takes place.

I. WHEN PRAYER IS DIFFICULT.

Because we are selfish by nature our prayers tend to center around ourselves. Even prayers of thanksgiving tend to be I-oriented. It is work to concentrate on others. Not that we should never pray for ourselves (what has been said earlier makes that clear), but we must spend a good share of our time interceding for the work of the kingdom of God.

Intercession is the most difficult form of our prayer work. Petition is prayer for ourselves (and that, too, is often difficult); but intercessory prayer for others requires far greater concentration. It takes energy and time to hold up to God specific requests, but there is rich reward in this kind of work.

HOW TO FACE THE CHALLENGES OF PRAYER

A. Praying for Full-Time Church Workers.

We often pray for the people now in the work of the church. We also pray for those preparing for full-time church work; these young people (and today, sometimes older people) are going through social, financial, and intellectual transition and sometimes spiritual transition. But do we intercede earnestly for *new* people to be called into tasks of ministry? Do we ask for people created by God for the specific purpose of kingdom work? Jesus said, "The harvest is plentiful, but the laborers are few; pray therefore the Lord of the harvest to send out laborers into his harvest" (Matt. 9:37–38). Apparently our prayers make a difference! Surely we cannot comprehend how our prayers could have any effect upon so important a matter (indeed, we cannot comprehend how our prayers *ever* have an affect). But Jesus' command would be irrelevant and meaningless if it were not so.

The chief handicap to Christian work is the existence of workers who have not been commissioned by God himself. Their work is of man; it is considered acceptable and even efficient in the eyes of men. But it is not of God. There are people on the mission field who never should have gone and people who are not there who ought to be. That situation Hallesby boldly declares "is our fault. We should have prayed. . . ." He says the same of pastors: We complain because of poor pastoral leadership but, "What we really should complain most about is ourselves and our slothfulness in prayer."[1] Think of the difference if every pastor were truly called, thrust out into the work of soul-winning and soul-nurturing as a result of God-motivated prayers. The effect upon the church and the world would be unspeakably great. (We have a hint of what would happen in the story of English Methodism under Wesley with his army of lay preachers, also in the account of the Moravian revival and the host of missionaries sent out from Germany.)

Moreover, we must pray fervently for God to raise up true teachers. The New Testament talks about the gift of

---

[1] O. Hallesby, *Prayer*, 26th ed. (Minneapolis: Augsburg, 1937), p. 69. This book has been of great help in the writing of this chapter.

teaching; this is a divine gift. It is the ability to communicate the moral and religious Law of God (righteous living) in the power of the Spirit. Our Sunday schools, Christian day schools, and church-related high schools and colleges must have teachers with this gift. Under inspired teaching the law of God is communicated in lower as well as higher education, in the physics as well as the Bible classroom, to the Christian as well as the unconverted. In the hands of a gifted instructor, teaching becomes a mighty instrument of evangelism and nurture. Let us pray earnestly for God to call and equip teachers in this New Testament sense.

Preachers of the gospel need our prayers. In times of success they are tempted to pride, power, and a certain ease. In times of failure they are tempted to discouragement, defeat, and a sense that they are unimportant. Our prayers would help to counteract these temptations. A retired missionary spent several months praying for every preacher and preacher's wife in his conference. There were beautiful results from those prayers. A seminary professor prayed by name for every student pastor each weekend; his particular burden was for their safety in travel. During those years not a single serious weekend accident took place.

May God raise up intercessors for our ministers.

B. Praying for Other Leaders.

Our leaders of civic organizations, of business, and of government have learned to stand alone. They often make decisions based upon their own wisdom, courage, and convictions. True, they have help from aides and committees. But in the last analysis they themselves must make the decisions and assume responsibility for them. Our leaders must sometimes make their decisions against the majority. This is not easy. They need the sheer strength and perseverance that comes from God. When the opposition moves in, when the community criticizes, when followers become disinterested, the leaders must carry on. Let us pray (1) for responsible leadership, (2) for their divine guidance and strength, (3) for an understanding and uncritical spirit on the part of ourselves. (This is not to suggest we should stand idly by in the presence of poor leadership. It is *irresponsible* criticism we must guard against.)

And let us not forget those we are prone to consider "lesser" leaders, who live selfless lives of beautiful service. In the little Swiss town of Jongy, in the canton of Vaud, lives a kindly parish worker who devotes her time to sick and convalescing children in the village hospital. She is surely a gift of God to her community. The children respond to her immediately—she is that type—and the comfort she gives to boys and girls and their parents simply cannot be measured. One of the parents rewarded her with some money. It never occurred to her to keep it for herself; she promptly announced that now she could buy certain toys she had wanted for the hospital nursery. As Christians we are obliged to hold these people before the throne of grace. We are also obliged to pray that more such helpers and leaders, possessing the gifts of grace, come forward for the work of God, the church, and the community.

Nor can we forget another category of leaders, the parents. They are without question the most important leaders! They form the opinions and ideals of our children and youth; they make or break our communities and our nation. As a rule, righteous people are made in the home, rarely apart from it. Pray that God will raise up parents who are true leaders of their children.

C. Praying for Worship Services.

Thank God for the fruit of our worship services; but think how much greater the fruitage if we would pray earnestly for them. The sermons might not be a great deal different, or again they might; at any rate we would be different in responding to them, and the unconverted would respond, too.

We do not need an outburst of emotionalism in our meetings. We know there is wholesome emotional response in conversion and deep religious experiences (as in all events of human life); but the usual work of the Spirit is in the quiet continuing program of the church. If the more dramatic revival comes, praise God. We need anything that truly will advance the kingdom. But let us leave the shape and expression of awakening up to God himself, for manmade efforts at "revival" are not genuine. At a recent week of evangelistic meetings in a progressive and evangelical college, I was impressed with the astute observation of the students themselves: "We are weary of repeated unhealthy 'emotional' experiences; but we do want authentic experiences." The quieter awakening sometimes continues long after its beginning, while the dramatic revival may end as quickly as it began . . . like an explosion. Let us pray earnestly that in the normal course of our church meetings, as well as in revivals, people will find God, be inspired to bring in outsiders, and be challenged to more righteous living. After all, just plain honest living with Christian joy may be the most potent human means of bringing people to God.

The best way to pray for your worship services is to become specific. List the unsaved in your community and circle of acquaintance, and beseech God for their salvation. Remember that *we are all the product of prayer*. Apparently no one is saved aside from someone's prayers. That is a sobering thought. Have you thought of the possibility of a poor lost soul who may have no one to pray for him? Have you thought further of the power daily prayer for unsaved individuals would generate? It would not be easy for the unrepentant to remain in their sins were they to be surrounded by the love and prayers of God's people.

There is absolutely no substitute for the work of prayer. How easy it is to let the prayer time slip by, to make excuses, even "legitimate" excuses. It is imperative that the Spirit of God "burn into our hearts this mystery, that the most important work we have to do is that which must be done on our knees, alone with God, away from the hustle of the world and the plaudits of men."[2] Prayer is that unique power which makes weak people the very channels of God to change the world. It is the great prerequisite and parallel necessity to all kingdom effort. If we had even a glimpse of

---

[2] Ibid., p. 80.

the value of prayer we would rise with new eagerness to the challenge of its work.

II. WHEN GOD SEEMS DEAF.

Chadwick confessed that his faith was most sorely shaken when a man died for whom he and his prayer partners firmly believed they had received assurance of healing. They fully expected his recovery. But he died. Mary and Martha must have felt the same about Lazarus, for they had informed Jesus of his illness, they had waited knowing full well his ability to heal. But he died. "Lord, if you had been here, my brother would not have died" (John 11:21). What had happened? Was Jesus deaf? Was he disinterested?

The answers to this inner wrestling are legion. But in the last analysis we must receive the answer or answers which meet our own individual needs. Perhaps the following thoughts will meet the needs of some.

A. Don't Quit Praying.

First, we cannot "throw in the sponge." We cannot say we suspected all along that prayer was a myth and that at last we have come to our mature senses. To give up faith in God is not the answer. Some people give up praying not so much in that definite, radical sense as in a way socially acceptable to their church group. They still go to church, bow their heads at prayer time, say grace before meals, but no longer engage in earnest believing prayer . . . because "once I prayed and believed but my prayer was not answered. God was quite deaf."

No! That cannot be our final answer. We may be tempted in that direction, but we dare not give in to that temptation. We must retain our firm belief that God is God, that he does all things well, that he is infinite in knowledge. God would not be so cruel as to play a trick on us. He is good, kind, and great; what he has done is for our larger benefit. And besides, we cannot see from his perspective, nor can we always see how natural law or the disobedience of another have played roles in the final outcome.

B. Believe God's Best Will Be Done.

Second, sometimes he wants to do something different (even better!) for us, something other than that for which we prayed in the first instance. Such was the case with Mary and Martha. It certainly had not occurred to them that their brother would be resurrected from the dead and that their lives would be thereby greatly and unbelievably enriched. And in addition, God was glorified the more. So it is with us. Frequently we are disappointed because God did not answer in *our* way; but his way is superior.

Very vivid to me is the experience of praying about a trip to the Holy Land. The plans were set with clarity of feeling and conscience. Months in advance of leaving I had received "assurance" that I would go. But at the last minute it was impossible to go. What had happened? Had God suddenly changed his mind? Was he now disinterested? Had I misread the Inner Voice? As it turned out, God had provided something different for that particular summer. He planned a period of rest, writing, reading, and meditation—all this in Switzerland with my family.

C. Reexamine the Motive of Your Prayer.

Third, only God-inspired prayers are answered. Said Glenn Clark, "I . . . announce a crazy paradox, that is, that none of *my* prayers has ever been answered. None of your prayers is ever answered. *Only God's prayers are answered.*" Naturally God will not respond to requests outside his own plan and purpose. To pray in the Spirit is to think God's thoughts after him.

D. Reexamine Your Attitudes.

We cannot expect to get answers when our hearts are so full of ungodly attitudes that we have no room for true prayers. Resentments or feelings of injury or insult cannot lodge in the heart alongside honest prayer. Nor can prayer live in a heart that refuses to accept circumstances ("if only things were different life would go right"). God cannot get at us if our hearts are not right, for these strong negative feelings drive him out.[3]

E. Don't Pray Too Much.

It *is* possible to pray too much. Olive Wyon tells of James Fraser's discovery of this truth. He was a missionary and one day lost his temper in the presence of the very people he was trying to work with. In his humiliation he attempted to find a reason for his poor behavior. He found he had prayed so long and seriously that he had actually robbed himself of exercise and fresh air. The cause was purely physical. He found, too, that depression was sometimes due to over-praying, that the cure was in setting himself to some task.[4] As someone has said, we function best spiritually when we function best physically. That is not a necessarily true statement, but it has its point. God can seem deaf because we have deadened the line through physical neglect.

F. Remember the Primary Purpose of Prayer.

God is more important than an answer to your prayer. Or rather, he *is* the answer. Said Oswald Chambers, "Whenever the insistence is on the point that God answers prayer, we are off the track. *The meaning of prayer is that we get hold of God, not of his answer.*" How can we get that truth into our thinking? By the regular experience of God in prayer. It is God we must have. Jesus made that clear when he said our Father knows what we have need of even before we ask (Matt. 6:8). A young seminarian missed our Lord's point entirely when he reasoned, "If God knows what I need already, and is prepared to meet my need, I need not pray." What happened to his devotional life is what you might expect: it disintegrated. The point of prayer is to get God. Answers are most meaningful when they are thought of least; prayer is most meaningful when God is thought of most.

---

[3] Cf. Olive Wyon, *Prayer* (Glasgow: Fontana, 1963), p. 91.
[4] Ibid., p. 92.

G. Admit That the Answer May Not Come.

Finally, let us face frankly that we will not always come even close to an answer. At times it seems so obvious that a certain prayer should be answered a certain way, but it is not. Search the Scriptures and our minds as we will, we cannot find a reason. In such case, let us not spend too much time trying to "figure it out." We can dissipate our energies in fruitless effort. God can grow dim, the heart cold. . . . This leads to the next situation in which praying Christians find themselves wrestling with a challenge.

III. WHEN CIRCUMSTANCES ARE AGAINST US.

Christianity and prayer are not mechanisms of escape from the cruel reality of a sinful and disturbing world. A significant error has been made by many of the Christian pulpit in broadcasting the idea that when one becomes a Christian he will have no more problems. Granted, it is rarely said that baldly; but the impression is nonetheless given.

This is not the model of life that Jesus presents to us. Jesus himself was known as the Man of Sorrows. Many of his disciples have followed in the footsteps of his suffering.

Donald Tweedie, Jr., says, "It has been a great mistake to identify Christian experience with a state of bubbling happiness free from mental stress." He goes on to say that there is surely no biblical base for this notion, that to the contrary the Scriptures are full of the conflicts Christians must face. He quotes H. G. Goodykoontz as saying point-blank that the "goal of life is not emotional tranquility." While the gospel offers comfort and rest it never glorifies peace-of-mindedness.[5]

When circumstances are against us, we may recoil at the thought of prayer. But the established Christian prays anyway. He knows that reverses will come and is therefore not surprised. They are normal in a sin-sick world. He will

---

[5]Donald F. Tweedie, Jr., *The Christian and the Couch, An Introduction to Christian Logotherapy* (Grand Rapids: Baker, 1963), pp. 25–26.

do what he can to eliminate sources of difficulty; what he cannot eliminate, he will use.

Now it is in the *use* of unhappy circumstances that the power of prayer comes into play. The inattentive Christian will let circumstances use him; the creative, praying Christian will use the circumstances for noble ends. That is the real secret of victorious praying. Defeat comes when we let circumstances determine our destiny. Jesus knew there would be no escape from the Cross, but he used it to redeem the world.

To tap the divine resources that make possible the use of pain, sufferings, and frustration requires a right relatedness to God. This relatedness is the gift of God that comes through prayer and is maintained by the same means.[6]

This leads us to say that the heart-cry of prayer is not for a life of ease, but to glorify God. "Not to us, O LORD, not to us, but to thy name give glory, for the sake of thy steadfast love and thy faithfulness!" (Ps. 115:1). God will give (or allow) ease when it glorifies him, but he will give (or allow) suffering when that glorifies him. Sometimes there is a lesson to learn. Sometimes we have become cocky in prayer, thinking we could order God. (What a marvelous thing that a weapon so powerful as prayer cannot be used for selfish, finite purposes!) It is when we pray according to his will and purpose that we have the assurance of a prayer being heard and answered. When we come to God in all humility and let him do with us as he pleases, when we ask him for guidance to use our circumstances (happy or unhappy) for his noble purposes, then it is that we are praying to glorify God.

IV. WHEN WE FEAR OUR YOUNG CHILDREN WILL NOT UNDERSTAND.

Perhaps you remember the account of the winged monkeys in *The Wonderful Wizard of Oz*. According to the story, if the lucky person who wears the Golden Cap says slowly,

---

[6]Perhaps the best page in E. Stanley Jones's *Abundant Living* is p. 275, where the secret of "Abundant Living 'In Spite Of' " is spelled out powerfully.

HOW ARE YOU PRAYING?

> Ep-pe, pep-pe, kar-ke!
> Hil-lo, hol-lo, hel-lo!
> Ziz-zy, suz-zy, zik!

then the monkeys will fly to the rescue. Whatever the wearer of the Cap asks the monkeys will do, even to the performing of superhuman feats.

We dare not teach a "winged monkey" theory of God to our children. He does not place at our disposal a fleet of angels who will deliver whatever we want when we say the "magic words" of prayer. Sometimes it is not in the best interests for us to have what we want; it may even be dangerous.

The story is told of a minister who had come home late and found pinned to his pillow a note that touched him deeply: "Dear Daddy, please, O please buy me a pair of roller skates." This was the climax of a long series of requests from his golden-haired daughter, so right then and there he went out to look for a pair. Though it was late he found a store open, made his purchase, and returned home to put the skates by his sleeping daughter. In the morning she went bounding in to her daddy even before he was awake, threw her arms around his neck and expressed her joy. She hurried out of the house to try her new skates. But an hour or so later, during the father's breakfast, neighbors brought in the dead body of his little girl. She had fallen backwards and had hit her head on the sidewalk. Imagine the pathos in the father's voice when he said, "If only I had known, if only I had known, I would never have purchased the skates were she to have pleaded endlessly." How was he to know so strange an accident would take place?

We simply do not know what is best for us. Our little children can understand something of that. They know they haven't all knowledge; they do know (if we have schooled them correctly) that God has all knowledge. When we pray we must qualify our asking in terms of what is best for us (and those around us, too). That is why we cannot have everything we ask. Besides, we might be spoiled if that were the case.

You see, this must be quite clear to the child who has a

natural capacity for gullible belief. "If God is great, if he answers prayers, then all I have to do is ask"—that is the faith of a little child. And it is a beautiful faith that we do not want to disturb, a faith which we as adults need more of. But that simple belief must be shaped by what we know of the nature of God and by what is good for the child himself.

As I write these words, a seven-year-old boy of our community has been unconscious or semi-conscious for weeks. He was struck by an automobile when he ran into the street after a ball. My six-year-old son has been concerned about his sick friend and has prayed for him at bedtime and often at meals. He repeatedly asks, "Daddy, will he be well soon? Will God heal him?"

What do parents say to a question like that? The answer cannot be an unqualified yes for obvious reasons. But the answer can and must be, "Yes, if it is God's will. God knows best, we do not." If our answers are not qualified by the will of God, they are neither scriptural nor sound. Think of the crisis in a child's mind if he has been assured of healing yet the healing does not take place. Nor is this a kind of convenient escape. Prayer conditioned by the will of God is scriptural and realistic.

V. WHEN OUR PRAYER ANSWERS ARE DELAYED.

"The best and most faithful intercessors I have met," says Professor Hallesby, "learned the holy art of intercession only after many trials or great suffering."[7] Often the art of prayer is learned (or partly learned) in a period of illness or suffering, for it is at those times especially that helplessness opens our hearts to the lessons of God. When life is going smoothly, a screen is erected between the individual and reality; but when difficulty comes, reality is exposed. God is seen in moments of realistic insight, and prayer becomes earnest with a crystal-clear honesty and sincerity.

Important lessons are learned in the delay of answers to

---

[7]Hallesby, *Prayer*, p. 165.

our prayers. We learn God has his own time; that he is sovereign; that we cannot command him. We learn patience, and we learn reliance upon him. These could not be learned if all our prayers materialized at the drop of a hat. "We do not know exactly when" our prayers will be answered, "but he who has learned to know God through the Spirit of God, has learned to leave this in His hands, and to live just as happily whether the answer arrives immediately or later."[8]

Sometimes we are afraid to pray because we fear God will require something difficult of us. There is some truth to that. It is dangerous to pray precisely because God does hear and answer prayer, and he may know that the pray-er himself is the one best qualified to bring about the answer.

Donald Tweedie, in *The Christian and the Couch*, points out that all efforts to avoid the truth will sooner or later catch up with us. He recommends meeting conflict head-on, even though this may seem more difficult at the moment. Direct confrontation "tends to maintain the unity of personality in the long run rather than to be divisive. This is another facet of the fact that 'the truth will make one free.' "[9] Now the same principle is at work in facing God. At times it seems more threatening to pray, but head-on confrontation of the situation with God is in the long term to our advantage and the advantage of the kingdom. Certainly God may require difficult things of us. Why not? We are his servants. But let us not refuse to pray on that account; let us face him in *his* power, seek in all honesty for his answer, and expect his strength in doing whatever he requires of us.

VI. WHEN OUR EFFORTS ARE NOT RECOGNIZED.

Prayer sometimes seems difficult because our prayer efforts are not recognized and appreciated. But the work of intercession is largely a private affair; it is done in secret where people do not see us, and most will never know the hours of work invested. Some believe that the work of intercession is the hardest work known to man; if that is so,

---
[8] Ibid., p. 128.
[9] Tweedie, *Christian and the Couch*, pp. 77–78.

why should we not be recognized? we ask. Perhaps the prevalence of that attitude is the reason God has a hard time finding intercessors. It is easy enough to get young people to work on a gospel team or to find a preacher who will mount a pulpit. But to be in the quiet of the prayer closet is quite a different matter.

When people for whom you have prayed are converted, in all probability the evangelist or pastor or someone else will be commended. No one will know of your work in prayer; you are unheralded. Jesus had a word for you who intercede in your own faithful way. He promised that "your Father who sees in secret will reward you" (Matt. 6:4). You already know his rewards (such as the release to God and things worthwhile), his mercies by day and night, the fellowship of keen praying Christians, and the answers to prayer that bring God closer to the people for whom you have interceded.

Professor Hallesby tells the story of old Jørn, servant on his father's farm in Norway. He suffered greatly from lack of natural endowments and from illness, but "little by little, in the school of difficult experiences, he learned the holy art of prayer." He prayed whenever he could, day or night, including by name people of his community. In due course people began to come to this simple man for counsel until the whole parish sought direction from him. His little hut was a center of spiritual healing. If he could not help, he could pray. "As the years passed, many a soul left his humble dwelling with a lighter tread and a happier heart."

In the final years of Jørn's existence he was very ill. Two devoted women cared for him; they said he would awaken in the night and pray aloud for individuals. He went from house to house, even mentioning children he had never met but who he knew had been born.

Hallesby recounts the beautiful incidents of his death and funeral. People vied with each other for the chance to be with him when he breathed his last; but "our Lord very neatly foiled them. . . ." He died with no witness; the one who was caring for him at the time had stepped out to the kitchen for a minute. At his funeral there gathered the largest crowd in the history of the little town, even though he had no relatives there. People stood at his coffin and wept as if they had lost a close relative; even the unconverted came and wept. In death he blessed others as he had done in life. "Both his life and his death were a fulfillment of the words of Scripture, 'Ask and ye shall receive.' "[10]

He blessed others. That is the greatest reward of intercessory prayer. It costs something to realize that reward.

VII. WHEN WE ARE CALLED UPON TO FAST.

Fasting was a normal part of the early Christian church, as even a cursory reading of Acts will indicate. Jesus himself prayed and fasted. But it is today a difficult business. Said a missionary: "I feel called upon to fast but find it most difficult. My wife fears for my health; what makes matters worse, she has never found it profitable for herself and thus cannot see the need of it."

But fasting is a powerful weapon. I know of a mother who fasted and prayed for the education of her son; it was a happy day indeed when she saw him graduated from university. Seasoned Christians know the advantages and results of fasting. But it is never easy. It requires wrestling with one's own desires and sometimes with the "sympathies" of one's family.

In what circumstances do we fast? Apparently when we need to. "Then the disciples of John came to him, saying, 'Why do we and the Pharisees fast but your disciples do not fast?' And Jesus said to them, 'Can the wedding guests mourn as long as the bridegroom is with them? The days will come, when the bridegroom is taken away from them, and then they will fast' " (Matt. 9:14–15). Indeed, the day did come, and then they did fast. But that was within the context of the specific, urgent needs of the early church.

Jesus gave strict warning against fasting to display piety: "And when you fast, do not look dismal, like the hypocrites, for they disfigure their faces that their fasting may be seen by men. Truly, I say to you, they have their reward. But when

---
[10] Hallesby, *Prayer*, pp. 166–67.

you fast, anoint your head and wash your face, that your fasting may not be seen by men, but by your Father who is in secret; and your Father who sees in secret will reward you" (Matt. 6:16–18). The hypocrite loses all the value of fasting because it is canceled by his pride.

The purpose of fasting is to center on things spiritual and eternal; also, it means to pray with the earnestness that comes with desperation. There is something about fasting that detaches one from the things of the world. Nor is this to say material things are bad; only pagan philosophies believe that. Christians believe food and other material things are the gifts of God, to be used in his service. That is clearly the New Testament position, as indicated for example in Romans 14:14 ("nothing is unclean in itself") and 1 Timothy 4:3 ("foods which God created to be received with thanksgiving"). But in the time of fasting, the mind is centered upon God and his ability to meet human need.

It is significant that Jesus fasted immediately after his baptism and during the period of his forty-day temptation (Matt. 4:2). Apparently one purpose of fasting is victory over temptation.

It is of further significance that Jesus prayed all night (no doubt without the physical refreshment food would bring) before he chose his disciples (Luke 6:12–13). This suggests that another purpose of fasting is to get guidance in the making of choices and decisions. Notice also Acts 13:2–3: "While they were worshiping the Lord and fasting, the Holy Spirit said, 'Set apart for me Barnabas and Saul for the work to which I have called them.' Then after fasting and praying they laid their hands on them and sent them off." It is no wonder the early church had the mind of God, so earnestly did they make their decisions. Notice again this scriptural principle of fasting before a choice: "And when they had appointed elders for them in every church, with prayer and fasting, they committed them to the Lord in whom they believed" (Acts 14:23).

FOR DISCUSSION

1. Why is prayer work? When is it work? Discuss, in turn, the work of prayer for new full-time church workers, for leaders, and for

church meetings. Itemize the kinds of church workers and leaders for whom we should pray.
2. Does God ever seem deaf to your prayers? Have you come to an answer(s) to this problem satisfactory to you?
3. Discuss the paragraph entitled "When Circumstances Are Against Us." Do you agree with Dr. Tweedie? What to you is the fundamental purpose of prayer?
4. Discuss ways of teaching children that the purpose of prayer is not just to get everything they want. You may want to share from your family experiences.
5. Do you think Professor Hallesby was right when he said that "most faithful intercessors . . . learned the holy art of intercession only after many trials or great suffering"?
6. Are we sometimes afraid of what God will ask us to do? Is it better to face God even when we fear what He will ask us to do? Explain.
7. Discuss fasting. What are its purposes? Do you care to share values of fasting from your own experience?

BIBLIOGRAPHY

Chadwick, Samuel. *The Path of Prayer*. London: Hodder and Stoughton, 1931. (See chap. 26, "The Problem of Unanswered Prayer.")
Hallesby, O. *Prayer*. 26th ed. Minneapolis: Augsburg, 1937.
Jones, E. Stanley. *Abundant Living*. New York: Abingdon, 1942.
Tweedie, Donald, Jr. *The Christian and the Couch: An Introduction to Christian Logotherapy*. Grand Rapids: Baker, 1963. (Some training in psychology is necessary to benefit from this book. It offers help in analyzing the dynamics of human personality, which of course is important for understanding the deeper levels of prayer.)
Wyon, Olive. *Prayer*. Glasgow: Fontana, 1962.

9
HOW TO PRAY FOR THE SPIRIT'S FULLNESS

"It is a verifiable phenomenon of Christian experience that an individual man [or woman], laid upon by the Spirit of God, can have his [or her] whole life lifted to a level of spiritual force and efficiency which previously would have seemed quite impossible."[1] That statement by James S. Stewart of Edinburgh can hardly fail to make its impact on us.

But our dilemma is just this: while we have no difficulty believing Stewart's truth for the apostles, for John Wesley, and others in history, or even for Billy Graham and other well-known Christians of our day, we hesitate to embrace the statement for ourselves. Yet surely Stewart's sentence rings true for ordinary people.

I. THE PERSONAL IMPACT OF THE SPIRIT'S INFILLING.

Permit me to speak from personal experience. Some years ago God gave me a friend, Ralph G. Turnbull, a Scottish-American minister of the gospel. In England he had come into contact with the Methodists, and partly through their influence had a crisis experience of Spirit-filling. Samuel

---
[1]James S. Stewart, *Thine Is the Kingdom* (Edinburgh: St. Andrews, 1956), p. 72.

Chadwick especially influenced him; Norman Dunning and W. E. Sangster, among others, touched his life, too. My Scottish friend's life radiated the Spirit so obviously—even during times of personal tragedy—that his very life set me to rethink my religious experience and made me conscious of God. Through the years he kept close contact with me and powerfully influenced my life. He gave me *The Testament of Samuel Chadwick, 1860–1932,* compiled by D. W. Lambert. I read that book with the deepest interest, and my attention was riveted to Chadwick's statement that early in his ministry he could say he had his education, preaching and teaching opportunities, and even saw a few souls come to Christ. In fact, confessed Sam Chadwick, at that time "I had everything but one thing, power." (Chadwick received the power of the Spirit one morning at a prayer meeting when praying, not for himself, but for revival.)

That statement got hold of me as nothing else had for perhaps half a dozen years. I hardly had the courage or objectivity to look into the mirror and ask, Do I—Donald E. Demaray—have the dynamic of which Samuel Chadwick spoke?

The next fifteen months I prayed more or less regularly, and frequently with intense earnestness, for the power of the Holy Spirit. But I really did not know that what I needed was the filling of the Spirit.

The last full week of August 1961 saw me in Winona Lake, Indiana, as a youth worker and teacher of young marrieds at a Bible conference. Three weeks earlier I heard a minister tell publicly the story of his Spirit-filling. At first skeptical, I soon recognized he was possessed of the same power to which Samuel Chadwick had referred, and the same dynamic that made possible the coping and spiritual achievement of my friend, Ralph Turnbull. (I had left that meeting under deep conviction, and from that moment entered a period I could accurately call desperate. I vowed not to cease seeking the Spirit until I found him. Actually, in all this he sought me and tried to get through pride and stubbornness to my inner being.)

On Tuesday night of the youth conference, Pastor Dale Cryderman preached a sermon on the Spirit-filled life. In that sermon he told the story of a minister who, three years before his death, experienced an anointing of God's Spirit that changed his ministry. The story struck me.

The next evening, Wednesday, was "Crusade Night." Young people who had gone to Ireland and Mexico shared their experiences. A young lady who traveled to Ireland commented, "I went an evangelical Christian; I returned an evangelistic Christian." That statement impacted me with great force.

Merv Russell, at that time an international youth director, gave the major message of the evening, and an impressive sermon it was. In it he told of leading a gospel meeting in Mexico City on the steps of a cathedral. At that point I was forced to confess inwardly that I did not have courage to hold a meeting out-of-doors.

I left that service praying that if possible my hunger for God would be satisfied. The Spirit of God led me so definitely that, as I look back, I am convinced he walked by my side. I walked across the Winona Lake convention grounds to the Billy Sunday Tabernacle, where Torrey Johnson had just finished preaching. I asked Dr. Johnson to pray with me. He seemed to know almost immediately what I needed, and for the first time I saw clearly God's desire. Dr. Johnson prayed the perfect prayer, referring tactfully to the pride of intellect, the folly of working in the energy of the flesh, and the naturalness of wanting the Spirit's fullness. At my request, he laid his hands on my head and prayed that I receive the fullness of the Spirit.

Now at first I did not recognize the Spirit. Frankly, I thought he had not done his work and that I would go on with the same gnawing hunger. But Torrey Johnson, sensing my concern, asked, "Were you converted by faith?" I got the message and in cold faith claimed the Spirit. I had not walked fifty paces out-of-doors until the Spirit of God bore witness with my spirit that he had in fact done the work.

Evidence of God's filling found confirmation beyond inward assurance—most particularly in helping people. With courage I bore witness about the fresh experience to a friend, a missionary on furlough from Egypt. I still recall with amazement how he responded. He commented that he himself needed the filling of God's Spirit; we prayed together and he found satisfaction. My work with the high school youth at the conference was another proof of changed ministry. Immediately young people responded to the gospel. And I cannot forget the girl, converted in a little church in her own town. She announced to me on the way into class on Saturday morning, "I and two other girls experienced Pentecost last night." Her eagerness to get back to her work as president of the youth group, and the obvious and complete sincerity with which she spoke, made clear the validity of her testimony.

On Sunday morning I had planned to complete a series of lectures for the young marrieds on the Christian home. But the inner voice of God insisted I change subjects; I must tell simply and straightforwardly what had happened to me. I began with my childhood Christian home, went on to conversion at age nine and a deeper dedication at eleven. Then I indicated that after earnest search God came to my life in a fresh and dynamic way August 24, 1961. At the end of that meeting I asked a minister friend to close in prayer, but upon completing his prayer, to the amazement of all, the service did not end; it had in fact only begun. The very man who prayed experienced the filling of the Spirit, stood to his feet and bore public witness to his newly found freedom. Another minister arose to say that for some twenty-five years he had sought the fullness of God and that that morning he had found it. Subsequently I received a letter from him in which he gave witness to a radical change in his pastoral work.

How many people found the full joy of the Lord that morning I do not know. A youth minister from Los Angeles, a college quartet singer, a varsity athletic player, a high school musician, a minister of the gospel who had been ordained an elder only a few weeks prior—these and others testified that they received the fullness of the Holy Spirit that day.

II. ITS BASIS IN PRAYER.

Prayer for the Holy Spirit indicates we are searching for him. God himself initiates that search; he creates the hunger.

A. God Initiates Prayer for His Spirit.

Charles Wesley caught this truth in a magnificent hymn he wrote for *Hymns of Petition and Thanksgiving*, published in 1746:

> No man can truly say
> That Jesus is the Lord
> Unless thou take the veil away,
> And breathe the living word;
> Then, only then we feel
> Our interest in His blood,
> And cry with joy unspeakable,
> Thou art my Lord, my God![2]

No one can force God's Spirit. God moves where and when and how he wills—that is a basic law of the spiritual life. Sometimes God speaks in crisis, at other times through a sermon, on yet other occasions by an act of kindness and love. God uses countless ways to initiate deep desire for him. The important factor is just this: He will create the hunger.

We can put ourselves in the way of that hunger by attending the means of grace like church attendance, group prayer experiences, openness in private devotion. We can do more: Ask questions of spiritually discerning people, read the devotional classics like Thomas à Kempis's *Imitation of Christ* and Brother Lawrence's *Practice of the Presence of God*,[3] and attend retreats and conferences where the atmosphere lends itself to spiritual breakthrough. But rest in this sure truth: To live in sincerity means God will come to you, adapting himself to your own individuality.

B. We Must Petition in Our Own Way.

God created us individually, and we come to him authentically only when we pray true to ourselves.

Quakers teach us the validity of individualism. Douglas

---

[2] Frank Whaling, ed., *John and Charles Wesley: Selected Prayers, Hymns, Sermons, Letters and Treatises* (New York: Paulist, 1981), p. 186.

[3] I have put these two devotional classics into contemporary language and format—à Kempis published in 1982 and Lawrence in 1976, both by Baker Book House of Grand Rapids, Mich.

V. Steere, writing in *Quaker Spirituality*, illustrates this truth by the story of President Chaim Weizmann of the new nation of Israel who came to the United States to thank President Truman for his quick recognition of the new state. Weizmann found Truman depressed. Truman complained that no matter what he did, some sector of America criticized him. "Mr. Truman, do you think that you are criticized?" Weizmann asked. "You ought to be in Israel. Here in the United States you are the president of two hundred million American citizens, but in Israel I am the president of a million presidents!" Dr. Steere adds to that story these apt words, "Quakers and Jews have much common ground in their individualism."[4]

Imitate no one in your prayers for God's full joy. He himself will direct your petitions as surely as he generates an appetite for himself. The spirit of mere imitation leads to abortive prayers. God in his sovereignty has quite enough power to shape the desires of your heart. Augustine summarized this well: "We come to God not by navigation but by love."[5]

C. Love Draws Us to Petition God for His Spirit.

God's instrument for creating hunger and shaping prayers is love. Thomas Merton observed that "love seeks one thing only: the good of the one loved." When we come alive to the truth that God wants only our good, we respond to him from our hearts. Christ sweeps away anger, fear, and guilt; love takes the place of self-defense. Precisely this is the Holy Spirit's cleansing and filling, for God is love and love is fear's opposite (1 John 4:18). Andrew Murray captures an important perspective on this truth in two sentences: "The love that we need is God Himself coming into our hearts.

---

[4] Douglas V. Steere, ed., *Quaker Spirituality: Selected Writings* (New York: Paulist, 1984), p. 3.
[5] Ibid., p. 4.

When the soul is perfected in love, it has such a sense of that love that it can rest in it for eternity. . . ."[6]

Let the Spirit of God draw you to himself as he will. A genuine glimpse of Calvary will melt your heart and bring you to your knees in effective petition.

D. We Experience the Crisis of Faith.

People often ask questions such as, What are my real motivations in wanting the Holy Spirit? Am I genuine or selfish? These questions loom important, for God will not answer insincere seeking. Humanly we would much rather have a bag of tricks to do eye-catching acts "for God" than shoulder the responsibilities of witness. Simon Magus in the Book of Acts (8:9–24) reminds us of badly motivated praying. Sometimes we must seek at some length until these self-oriented desires come to an end. E. Stanley Jones believed the 120 tarried in the Upper Room for days because "it takes a long time for some people to surrender."

And just there lies the secret: surrender, whether it takes one minute or ten days. When we actually give up ourselves to the Lord Jesus, in that moment he fills us with his empowering Spirit. God is in business to help us come to that point of authenticity, and he will by our full cooperation. He even gives us grace to cooperate with him.

That cooperation ultimately involves stepping over the doubts and questions to believe God really is helping us to surrender ourselves. We take his gift of surrender quite by faith, even cold faith, never minding feelings. Feelings can come and go, observes C. S. Lewis, but God's love remains stable.[7]

Sometimes we must cooperate with God by locating Scripture promises like John 7:38 or Acts 2, even putting our name and date in the margin of the Bible passage. Some of us need to "nail it down" as a symbol of active faith, then

---

[6] Merton and Murray quotations from Sherwood Eliot Wirt and Kersten Beckstrom, eds., *Topical Encyclopedia of Living Quotations* (Minneapolis: Bethany House, 1982), p. 148.

[7] C.S. Lewis, *Mere Christianity* (Glasgow: William Collins' Sons, 1955), p. 115.

return to the promised passage in times of doubt to restore full confidence that God has in fact done his work.

Faith is a gift. It is also like a muscle and develops girth with exercise. You will find faith growing, sometimes quickly and sometimes more slowly, as you walk in the fullness of the Spirit across the months and years.

III. AND WHAT ABOUT FRESH FILLINGS?

Yes. A resounding yes. Paul said he died daily; that means he experienced fresh fillings of the Spirit of Christ regularly, for death to selfishness is always the door to freedom. Renewals come commonly to sincere Christians. These new experiences of God we call "anointings." Often he comes to us again in this manner to gird us for a special task that lies ahead, as he did with a certain woman who found strength just before a personal crisis and a college president-elect who drew closer to God in preparation for his enormous administrative assignment.

We pray for fresh contacts with God when we know we need them. That college president sensed his desperate need after his election. But often we do not know what lies ahead, like the woman who could not have known the personal crisis around the corner. God may come in very special ways and at times we least expect him. Always say yes to him when he arrives at your soul's door. Sometimes he comes, not due to a pending crisis, but simply because he loves you and likes your company!

The one who stays near to God in Scripture reading, prayer, and the other means of grace will know frequent touches of his Spirit.

DISCUSSION

1. What do you mean by the infilling of the Spirit? Cite some Scripture passages.
2. Have you experienced your personal Pentecost? Is that experience still fresh and meaningful?
3. If asked to share your testimony concerning the Holy Spirit, what would you say?

4. How do you believe Christians should teach the fullness of the Spirit?
5. How does freedom and joy in the Spirit relate to personal fulfillment?

BIBLIOGRAPHY

Demaray, Donald E. *The Imitation of Christ.* Grand Rapids: Baker, 1982.(A paraphrase of the work by Thomas à Kempis.)
_____. *The Practice of the Presence of God.* Grand Rapids: Baker, 1975. (A paraphrase of the work by Brother Lawrence.)
Jones, E. Stanley. *Abundant Living.* Nashville: Abingdon, 1976.
_____. *Christ of the Indian Road.* Nashville: Abingdon, 1930.
_____. *Victorious Living.* Nashville: Abingdon, 1936.
Marshall, Catherine. *Beyond Our Selves.* Lincoln, Va.: Chosen Books, 1981.
Smith, Hannah W. *The Christian's Secret of a Happy Life.* Springdale, Pa.: Whitaker House, 1983.
Steere, Douglas V., ed. *Quaker Spirituality: Selected Writings.* New York: Paulist, 1984.
Whaling, Frank, ed. *John and Charles Wesley: Selected Prayers, Hymns, Sermons, Letters and Treatises.* New York: Paulist, 1981.

10

ESPECIALLY FOR MINISTERS AND PRAYER GROUP LEADERS

In this chapter we shall look at three basic aspects of prayer leadership: (1) the leader's prayer life, (2) the leader's prayers for others, and (3) the leader's prayers with others.

I. THE CHRISTIAN LEADER'S LIFE OF PRAYER.

Evelyn Underhill says, "the only real apostolic life" is the life of prayer, which is a man "in the deeps of his soul attached to God." Each Christian begins with a chance of experiencing this deeper life in God, "but only a few develop it." What is more, "the laity distinguish in a moment the clergy who have it from the clergy who have it not."[1] What is true of clerical is true of lay leadership, especially leadership of our prayer groups. We cannot fool our people; they know whether or not we are people of prayer. They know. It will do no good to preach piously at our people to pray if we do not lead the way. That is one reason the entrance into, and habitual practice of, the life of prayer is absolutely essential.

The essence of "the only real apostolic life," the life of prayer, is yielding to God. If we become lax and hit-and-miss instead of regular, this is only because our wills are not fully

---

[1] *Concerning the Inner Life,* quoted in Douglas V. Steere, "Spiritual Renewal in Our Time," *Union Seminary Quarterly Review,* November 1961, p. 41.

yielded to God. There can be no other reason. Even on those days when we are too weary to "concentrate" on God, we must come into his presence just to be there. Development is taking place whether we sense it at the moment or not. The same is true of those prayer periods when, though we are not especially weary, it seems "nothing is happening"; when prayer experience is a kind of blank. But something *is* happening. That is why E. Stanley Jones says, "Prayer is always right, with or without an emotional content."[2]

"The worst sin," said P. T. Forsyth, "is prayerlessness." Yielding to God is the opposite of prayerlessness; indeed, it is prayer. This yieldedness is so essential for our prayer leadership.

"What," asks W. E. Sangster, "was the secret" of Forbes Robinson's "extraordinary spiritual power?" His answer is "love and prayer."[3] Is it then any wonder that the quiet time is imperative? "Give up work if need be," says one urgent minister of the gospel. "Your influence finally depends upon your own firsthand knowledge of the unseen world. . . ."[4]

You see, the very qualities of prayer leadership are born in prayer; they can be born nowhere else! That love of our people which reflects a genuine inner sympathy, tact, insight, and joy is the product of communion with God. This leads us to say that what you *are* is shaped by your life of prayer. We often hear the cliché, "What you are speaks louder than what you say." With a good application St. John of the Cross said that about Christians; he declared that their very beings revealed their spirituality. The actual words Christians use are not as persuasive as we tend to think; it is what is behind the words, namely a *Christian life*. Leslie Davison puts it this way: "It is the way we speak as much as what we say, the warmth or coldness of our approach . . . our spontaneous asides . . . our willingness to help. . . ."[5]

Speaking to ministers, Dick Sheppard said, "It is beyond

---

[2] E. Stanley Jones, *How to Pray* (reprinted from *The Christian Advocate*), p. 12.
[3] W. E. Sangster and Leslie Davison, *The Pattern of Prayer* (London: Epworth, 1962), p. 118.
[4] Ibid., p. 119.
[5] Ibid., p. 123.

dispute the business of every parson to transform his own life until all unconsciously it is capable of giving out the same kind of music that Jesus made in Galilee." Then with fine insight he adds: "We are never abused or laughed at for being like Him. We are discounted because we are so unlike Him." So it is that the people we lead want to see the spirit of Jesus; if he is to be seen in us, obviously we must spend time with him.

When our people see him, they will get a sure word from God. Our people want that sure word they see in Jesus. They want it badly. They do not long for "profundity"—they feel that is beyond them—but they do want a certain message from heaven.

James S. Stewart refers to a "most moving scrap of conversation" in George Macdonald's *Robert Falconer:* " 'If I only knew that God was as good as that woman, I should be content.'

" 'Then you don't believe that God is good?'

" 'I didn't say that, my boy. But to know that God was good and kind and fair—heartily, I mean, and not half-ways with ifs and buts. My boy, there would be nothing left to be miserable about.' "[6]

That certain knowledge with no ifs and buts may come in those rare moments of insight when reading a book, listening to a sermon, hearing a great piece of music, or being out in nature. But doesn't it come more often in an encounter with a Christian person?

The awareness of that depth of spirituality in another Christian's life comes not so much from the circumstances in which he lives (they may be ordinary or not). Nor is it rooted in what that person says or the way he says it. It is surely not that the "hearty" Christian is trouble-free. But he knows God, and in his own surety you become sure. Someone has said that a saint dwells "with reiteration on commonplaces with which you were perfectly well acquainted before you were twelve . . . but you must make allowance for him, and remember that the knowledge, which is to you" superficial is

---

[6]James S. Stewart in *The Gates of the New Life* (New York: Charles Scribner's Sons, 1940).

to him "solid." It is that "solid" knowledge, that sure word from and about God, that our people want.

E. M. Bounds has made classic his descriptions of great praying leaders, people who had this "solid" know-so faith.[7] Charles Simeon, he says, spent the hours of 4:00 A.M. till 8:00 A.M. with God. John Wesley gave two hours daily, and someone said of him, "He thought prayer to be more his business than anything else, and I have seen him come out of his closet with a serenity of face next to shining." John Fletcher "stained the walls of his room by the breath of his prayers." He would even pray all night sometimes. Luther said, "If I fail to spend two hours in prayer each morning, the devil gets the victory through the day. I have so much business I cannot get on without spending three hours daily in prayer." One of Luther's mottos was, "He that has prayed well has studied well."

Bounds continues his galaxy of pray-ers:

Someone said of Archbishop Leighton that "prayer and praise were his business and his pleasure." Of Bishop Ken it was said his soul was "God-enamored." Bishop Francis Asbury proposed "to rise at four o'clock as often as I can and spend two hours in prayer and meditation." Samuel Rutherford got up at 3:00 A.M. for prayer, Joseph Alleine at 4:00. Robert Murray McCheyne found that the hours from six to eight were best for him for morning prayers. He had other times of prayer during the day, too.

It is unbelievable but true that John Welch thought a day poorly spent if he had not given eight to ten hours to prayer. In the night hours he threw around him a tartan blanket. His wife often complained, but he replied, "O woman, I have the souls of three thousand to answer for, and I know not how it is with many of them!" Bishop Wilson found that the most striking thing in Henry Martyn's journal is "the spirit of prayer, the time he devoted to the duty, and his fervor in it." Payson wore grooves into the floor where he knelt habitually. "To his ardent and persevering prayers must no doubt be

---

[7] E. M. Bounds, *Power Through Prayer* (Chicago: Moody), pp. 38–42.

ascribed in a great measure his distinguished and almost uninterrupted success."

The Marquis de Renty ordered his servant to summon him after half an hour of prayer, but looking through a keyhole the servant saw the moving expression on his master's face and could not disturb him. Another half hour passed, and still the servant could not bring himself to rouse him. Finally after an hour and a half he called; when the master got up from his knees he commented upon the shortness of the half hour!

Missionary David Brainerd said, "I love to be alone in my cottage, where I can spend much time in prayer." William Bramwell, early Methodist, spent hours on his knees, almost lived there, but he "went over his circuits like a flame of fire." He often spent as much as four hours at one time in prayer. Bishop Andrewes invested about five hours daily in prayer and meditation. Sir Henry Havelock spent his first two hours every day in prayer. Earl Cairns was up at six to have an hour and a half of Bible study and prayer before breakfast. Judson, who opened the work in Burma, said, "Leisurely devote two or three hours every day not merely to devotional exercises but to the very act of secret prayer and communion with God." Seven times every twenty-four hours he prayed, beginning after midnight "amid the silence and darkness of the night," then at dawn, then at nine, twelve, three, six, and nine. "Be resolute in His cause. Make all practical sacrifices to maintain it. Consider that thy time is short and that business and company must not be allowed to rob thee of thy God." We may call Judson a fanatic, but he opened Burma to the gospel!

That is Bounds's array of men of prayer. Think how many could be added to his list. The missionary James Fraser, pioneer in China and Burma; George Müller, who established an orphanage—or rather, orphanages!—in Bristol, England, where he fed and clothed the children by prayer. But you are saying, "I cannot pray like that; I am a busy man [or homemaker]. And if I had leisure, I haven't the gift of much prayer." Whether you are like Mrs. Billy Graham, who does most of her praying "on the hoof," or like the seamstress in my community who has risen at 5:00

ESPECIALLY FOR MINISTERS AND PRAYER GROUP LEADERS

A.M. for years, God has a prayer life tailored for you. Find it and let it—or rather him—mold you and develop your gifts for his service.

II. THE LEADER'S PRAYER FOR OTHERS.

W. E. Sangster's Westminster Pamphlet No. 4 is dedicated to "Twelve Ways of Service." He exhorts us to cultivate the qualities of neighborliness, hospitality, citizenship, and others. But his twelfth and last suggestion is prayer, and of this he says, "it is the most powerful of all forms of service." He claims that nothing surpasses it in influence and that nothing can equal it. "In heaven we shall see that the men and women of influence in every age were the men and women mighty in secret intercessory prayer."[8] That is a fact not difficult for mature Christians to believe.

Intercessory prayer as such has been dealt with elsewhere so need not be pursued here, only to say that it is easier to be neighborly, hospitable, or a good citizen than it is to spend some honest time in intercession. The reason may be that "every other form of service is noticed by someone," and surely this is why Sangster says it is "the most unselfish of all forms of service."[9]

Every prayer leader—especially pastors—should read Charlie W. Shedd's book, *How to Develop a Praying Church*,[10] for it contains the beautiful story of how hundreds of people in a local church were engaged in intercessory prayer. Shedd was pastor of a church in Houston, Texas, at the time he wrote that book, and there he learned how to involve a high percentage of his people in private and group prayer. He developed a prayer program with 250 undershepherds in his church. At first the only requirement was that each undershepherd pray daily for the families (no more than four) under his care. It was understood that this meant remembering each member of each family. But soon the undershepherds wanted to make personal contact with the people for

---
[8] W. E. Sangster, *Twelve Ways of Service* (London: Epworth, 1956), p. 18.
[9] Ibid., pp. 17–18.
[10] New York: Abingdon, 1964.

whom they were interceding. Some called in homes; some asked prayer for themselves; others shared devotional materials. Out of this developed the fine idea of having each undershepherd calling in every home under his care once a quarter to deliver the denomination's devotional guidebook. To make the intercessions relevant and vital, undershepherds were informed of illnesses or emergencies. Some very touching and beautiful experiences came out of the program.[11] The undershepherd promised to do five things:
1. Pray daily for each member of his flock.
2. Deliver the quarterly devotional guidebook to his homes.
3. Minister to the needs of his people.
4. Check attendance of his "sheep" each Sunday.
5. Encourage his people to attend the "Lessons in Discipleship" (local church classes set up to inspire prayer and genuine churchmanship).

Here is a concrete program of intercession and follow-through which commends itself by its workability. The undershepherds don't expect their work to be recognized so much as realized; their reward is in seeing people helped and encouraged. Knowing them personally, in joys and in trials, makes intercession the more meaningful.

Prayer leaders are priests—that is, mediators between their people and God. In true intercession the leader bridges that gulf; he prostrates himself over the abyss that separates God and man and becomes the "live wire" that feeds spiritual power into the souls of the members of his prayer group or church circle. Put in your prayer notebook the names of each person in the group you lead. Pray for them daily, at least every day or two. If you are a pastor and find it difficult to get around to all your people, divide them by geography or alphabetically (or whatever way is most convenient), and in this way intercede for them all every three weeks or so. There is nothing that will bring us close to our people and their specific needs like this kind of disciplined intercession. Included in our intercessions must

---
[11] Ibid., chap. 5.

be thanksgiving for the very fact that God has given us people to lead, help, and pray for. That they are there, available for direction or fellowship or both, is something for which to be profoundly grateful.

Then, let us not forget to pray for the wider world. The nineteen wealthiest nations in the world hold 16 percent of the world's people and two-thirds of the world's money! The fifteen poorest nations hold half the world's people and only 9 percent of the world's money.[12] Let that fact bore its way into your thinking. Meditate upon the inequality of the world. Note that this is a very real and basic cause of the world's unrest. See how it is impossible for the world to go on this way much longer.

From there let your mind move to the worldwide missionary program. What can you do to help that enterprise? If you are a young person, ask, Is God calling me to missionary service? If not, can I give more money, pray more faithfully for the missionaries I know? What can I do? Concentrate upon the lost of the world until your heart aches and burns to see them saved from sin and poverty.

Pray also about the evangelism of the world, the nation, and your own neighborhood. An excellent method of prayer at this point is to go through Sangster's fifteen-page Westminster Pamphlet, *Twelve Ways of Evangelism*. He discusses them all—personal evangelism, preaching evangelism, visitation evangelism, open-air evangelism, and so on. List the people you know who are involved in the various kinds of evangelism. Pray for them earnestly. Ask yourself in what avenue of evangelism you ought to be working; all praying Christians should be active in some type of program to bring the lost to Christ.

Then do not overlook your local church. On your knees talk with God about such pertinent questions as these: Is our church God's instrument for producing good (righteous) men and women? Are we doing anything to change our community for the better? What is our church doing for children, youth, young marrieds, the middle-aged, the

---

[12] Sangster, *Twelve Ways of Service*, p. 13.

elderly? for the women? the men? for the erring and imprisoned? for those who do not attend church services? for the widows and the suffering? From these questions, move to thanksgiving for what *is* being done in these areas: for the Sunday school with its teachers and superintendents; for those genuinely converted, changed from a life of apathy or sin to vital living in Christ; for the young married Sunday school class; for the men's organization and the women's missionary society; and the list could go on. For all these and more you will want to thank God. By the time you have gone this far in your prayers for your local church, you will have seen definite areas of need, gaps that should by all means be filled. As the Spirit brings these to mind, list them; eventually this may develop into conversations with your pastor or a keen layman, and finally to fruitful action.[13]

Intercession is a key to effective prayer leadership.

III. THE LEADER'S PRAYER WITH OTHERS.

Prayer *with* others does of course involve praying *for* others. One is generally in private while the other is social. Here we want to single out some of the situations in which we have the opportunity to pray with others, and also examine briefly the needs of our people, those basic urges that call us to prayer and concern for them.

What are some of the situations in which we find ourselves praying with other people?

A. Within Prayer Groups.

Group prayer has been discussed in chapter 4. Here it need only be reiterated that there is really no substitute for the prayer cell. If God is talking to you about starting cells in your church or leading an existing prayer group, by all means respond. This is one key to revival and to involving our people. The value to the participants is of course beyond measure; more important, God is pleased because he made

---

[13] For excellent prayer guidance and stimulation to local church action, see W. E. Sangster, *A Check-Up for Our Church*, Westminster Pamphlet No. 2 (London: Epworth, 1956).

us for fellowship with him. One saint of church history confided that she met on occasion with four others for the "purpose of undeceiving each other, for conferring on the means of reforming ourselves, and of giving God the greatest pleasure." Meditate on those reasons for small group prayer; they are solid.

One word of warning: In the leadership of small prayer groups we must refrain from that over-pious attitude which falsely remakes every item of our lives "spiritual." This gets old sooner or later (usually sooner) and drives people away from the group. Theresa of Avila cried, "From silly devotions, Oh Lord, deliver us." For the Christian there is a sense in which there is no difference between the sacred and the secular, so why spiritualize everything? The normal Christian life is sacred already.

B. During Visitation.

The pastoral call is surely the occasion for prayer with God's people and those who have met tragedy or difficulty of any type. I knew a pastor who called systematically, up and down the blocks in his community, and at the end of each call he knelt down and prayed. You will have to judge the wisdom of that, but surely when one goes to call on his own people he should not leave, except in unusual circumstances, without prayer. There is always comfort and inspiration in the pastoral prayer, especially in the intimate setting of the home. Of the factors that go into making a pastoral call quite distinct from a social visit, surely prayer heads the list. Dr. Sangster made this point in print during the year he was president of the Methodist Conference in Britain. He was surprised at the vehement response of a few clergy. They not only differed with him, they were angry. They offered no real reasons for failing to make a practice of prayer in their calls—"only plain and undisguised annoyance. It has remained in a corner of my memory over the years as one of the minor mysteries of my presidential term."[14] I should think it would!

---

[14] Sangster and Davison, *Pattern of Prayer*, p. 120.

HOW ARE YOU PRAYING?

Our lay leaders of church groups—especially prayer groups—should develop the art of prayer in visitation situations. Why not? We know our people by having met with them week after week in the group; and there can be no doubt that the prayer, properly timed and said, will be warmly appreciated. Develop the gift of verbal prayer in the visitation situation. The reader is directed once more to Charlie Shedd's *How to Develop a Praying Church*, especially chapters 4 and 5, which tell of laymen in roles of prayer leadership.

Hospital visitation requires some skill and knowledge. Some people are afraid of doctors and hospitals; these patients need assurance which we can help give them. Many are depressed; most are sensitive to loud talking and laughing. They are in no mood for fast conversation. Thus the call must have about it the atmosphere of calm, rest, and concern (without being grave). Talk in low tones and at a quiet rate. Ask if there is anything you can do: "May I take a message to your home? bring something to the hospital you particularly need or would like?" You can lift a considerable load by a simple act of kindness. Since the patient has time on his hands, he may think seriously—perhaps for the first time in his life—about the meaning of life and death. At any rate, the conversation can take any turn, and you will know when he has talked as long as he wishes (which may be long or short).

The hospital prayer, too, must be in quiet, reassuring tones. You may be praying in a ward of six or eight people. (Sometimes others will see you praying and invite you to minister to them. That is a rich opportunity.) In your prayer you may want to mention things indicated in your conversation just concluded. By all means include something to the effect that the patient is in God's kind and loving care, and that healing comes from God. If death seems possible, even probable, you will sense from the situation how to form your prayer in such a way as not to frighten the patient but to put him at ease and once more in God's hands.

Ministers usually have access to a patient at any time, day or night; laymen must come at calling hours. Sometimes the best thing a layman can do is send a card, note, or

ESPECIALLY FOR MINISTERS AND PRAYER GROUP LEADERS

flowers. The minister is trained in hospital visitation and knows what to do. A blundering call can be untimely, even harmful. But whether it seems most appropriate to go in person or by letter, nothing will be so comforting as to know that his church and prayer group are remembering him.

C. In Professional Contacts.

Prayer is appropriate and appreciated in an amazing variety of situations. You will sense by the tone of the situation and conversation what is appropriate. I know a lawyer who locks his door and prays with his clients in the office. The Christian professional man in an office has a context of privacy in which to bless his people with prayer. This is true of college teachers and administrators, especially those in an evangelical institution of learning. Sometimes it will be right to pray with a burdened soul on the street, in a restaurant booth, or over the telephone.

The principle surely is this: Anywhere and any time is appropriate for prayer with another person, provided the right conditions are present, and they often are. School yourself in that sensitivity to the Spirit by which he will indicate when and where and with whom to pray. None of us can ever know the actual help that may come to the one with whom we pray, but the Holy Spirit knows.

D. Reasons to Pray With Others.

Now let us look at some reasons for prayer, some very basic needs of our people. If we identify these, we will better know how to pray with others. *Holiness* is one of these fundamental needs. Albert Camus spoke for us all when he had one of his characters say, "What interests *me* is to know how one can become a saint!" That's it! We want to know how to become truly good, holy. God has made us for himself and we are unhappy until we find him; finding God is a lifetime affair, and part of that finding is growing more and more like him. That is what the quest for sanctity, sainthood, holiness—whatever you want to call it—is all about. Some call it perfection, which Olive Wyon has beautifully defined as follows: "'Perfection' ... does not mean an impossible purity or blamelessness, but rather the idea of 'completion.' In other words, we are meant to go on to maturity. Holiness is simply 'the flowering of Christian growth and development.' " In this developing wholeness is found the deepest satisfactions in life. It is the fulfillment we are made to seek until we find. "Thoughtful people are tired of living distracted, divided lives; they want a unifying principle, and an aim," says Miss Wyon.[15] We long for wholeness, completeness. That is why the artist wants to make a "finished" painting, or the composer a "satisfying" piece of music. We have that drive for what the psychologist calls "integration," and the Christian believes it is found in God. If after conversion we are not constantly moving on toward integration or holiness, conversion has probably lost its meaning. The chief end of holiness is fellowship with God, and a secondary end is helping to right the wrongs of society. In other words, holiness is both spiritual and ethical.

To be holy is to be like Christ, who sets the standards of spirituality and behavior. Christ lived a selfless life—in that is a clue to the meaning of personal holiness or completion. Another clue is in the love chapter, 1 Corinthians 13, which describes many of the characteristics that Christ exemplified. Still other clues are found in the narrative of Jesus' ministry which we read in the Gospels.

Related to the basic human urge for holiness is the drive toward *fulfillment*. Indeed, the two are very closely related. Few realize that spiritual fulfillment is the key to life fulfillment, that the one brings the other. Most think that the "perfect" job, the right working conditions, more money—any number of things—will bring fulfillment. That is a half-truth as can be plainly seen by the restlessness of our affluent yet dissatisfied society. Everywhere we turn, people are reaching out for some meaning in life. And one of our leading theologians has said that all human problems can be reduced to three: death, suffering, and *meaninglessness*. Life has its greatest meaning when fulfillment is most complete.

---

[15] *On the Way* (London: SCM Press, 1958), in the chapter, "The Way of Holiness."

ESPECIALLY FOR MINISTERS AND PRAYER GROUP LEADERS

When we understand that we are the most normal when in true prayer, we begin to see the clue to personal fulfillment and meaning. Prayer, someone has said, "is the God-relationship that makes a man a man." We are created by God to be God-oriented. To orient ourselves to public opinion, the "dream" world of better days ahead, or good feelings is to be adjusted (or rather maladjusted) around the wrong things. Fulfillment will never come in that way.

Fulfillment comes through a process of spiritual growth. P. T. Forsyth cried, "How is it that the experience of life is so often barren of culture for religious people? They become stoic . . . but not humble; they have keen sight but not insight. . . . They have no spiritual history. . . . At sixty, they are, spiritually, much where they were at twenty-six. . . . They do not face themselves, only what happens to them." There you have it! The gross ignorance of spiritual things within the precincts of church fellowship! It does not seem possible that people who attend church and listen to the preacher each week are still without that quality of spiritual growth so necessary to fulfilled living. They would not think of being so ignorant about their business, their family, their hobby. But about fellowship with God—that is a different matter! Why? One searches in vain for valid reasons. When the means of grace are so available, why is spiritual lassitude so common?

As prayer leaders, we are obliged to lead our people into the paths of genuine spiritual progress.

Then people want to know the meaning of *suffering*. This comes to us, not so much in cut-and-dried theological explanations, as in the very stuff of experience. Fritz Kunkel confided to a group of friends that he had been "pulled into a state of inward clarification and openness by his missing arm which he lost in the First World War."[16] Here is a perfect example of the "ministry" of suffering. Suffering is a gift which, if properly used, will bring us along the road to maturity. It can help us find ourselves and our place in society. A man who had suffered a great deal said to Brian

---

[16]Steere, "Spiritual Renewal," p. 40.

Sternberg, the young pole vaulter who was paralyzed in a trampoline accident, "You and I have had the privilege of suffering."

"To some," said E. Stanley Jones, God "entrusts the ministry of suffering. . . . "[17] (Jones's *Abundant Living* is replete with illustrations of how suffering can be used for the glory of God [see pp. 283–86].) It is hard and sometimes impossible to communicate that truth to a person in the throes of tragedy. But if one knows the truth himself, it will be of help in prayer leadership and will "leak" out at just the right time and place. Perhaps someone else can say it better than we.

Then we must be available to pray for our people in *death*. Bishop William Pearce was asked, toward the end of his long and fruitful ministry, "What would you do if you were to start your ministry over again?" His answer was simple yet profound: "I would love my people." Obviously he meant that for all of life—in times of joy as well as sadness—but is that not the best we can do for people when they experience death? God's love for us is the basis for that. Said Meister Eckhart, a German mystic of centuries past, "God is foolishly in love with us. It seems He has forgotten heaven and earth and deity" and gone to loving me. As prayer leaders, we are the channels to express that marvelous love of God. How do we do that in the hour of death?

For one thing, just being there and listening can be as communicative of love as anything else we might do. The bereaved person has a great deal invested in the lost loved one. In the case of an invalid, care has been invested, perhaps over a long period of time. In the case of a child, careful home rearing has been invested. One of the laws of human nature is that those things or people in which we have the most invested will elicit our greatest response. Frequently that response takes the form of verbal expression, so to listen attentively to that story may be the best service we can render at the hour of need.

Sometimes we can be of great service to the bereaved

---

[17] E. Stanley Jones, *Abundant Living* (New York: Abingdon, 1942), p. 286.

ESPECIALLY FOR MINISTERS AND PRAYER GROUP LEADERS

simply by sharing the experience of grief. An author produced his monumental work and won acclaim, but remained sad. He confided, "Yes, it is grand, but my wife is not here to share it." So another way we might love our people is by a visit at a time when we can be a "substitute" for sharing the experiences that once were shared by the deceased. Other ways are common knowledge: flowers, a card or letter of sympathy, the running of an errand—anything to let the love of God shine through.

The quest for holiness, for fulfillment, for the understanding of suffering, for the love of an understanding person in death—these are some of the most basic needs of mankind. To understand these, even in an elementary sort of way, is of help in making us better prayer leaders. If we truly love God, faithfully store his Word in our hearts, and acquire the gift of availability—these will go a long way in the further development of leadership.

BIBLIOGRAPHY

Bounds, E. M. *Power Through Prayer*. Chicago: Moody, n.d.
Jones, E. Stanley. "How to Pray," *The Christian Advocate*.
Sangster, W. E. and Leslie Davison. *The Pattern of Prayer*. London: Epworth, 1962.
————. The Westminster Pamphlets, especially No. 2, *A Check-Up for Our Church*; No. 3, *Twelve Ways of Evangelism*; and No. 4, *Twelve Ways of Service*. London: Epworth, 1956.
Shedd, Charlie W. *How to Develop a Praying Church*. New York: Abingdon, 1964.
Steere, Douglas V. "Spiritual Renewal in Our Time," *Union Seminary Quarterly Review*, November 1961.
Wyon, Olive. *On the Way*. London: SCM Press, 1958.

INDEX

Alleine, Joseph 155
Asbury, Francis 3, 13, 90, 155
Baillie, John 25, 33, 42, 43, 73
Baptism 58, 81, 82, 94, 95, 141
Barclay, William 22, 25
Beethoven, Ludwig von 34
Belief 15, 37–39, 57, 93, 95, 99, 131, 137
Bible 7, 10, 12, 13, 15–17, 19, 22, 23, 25, 30, 33, 36, 57, 63, 64, 68, 69, 71, 78–84, 86, 88, 89, 92, 95, 102, 109, 117, 122–24, 128, 144, 149, 150; Bible study 15, 57, 64, 69, 124, 156
Boldness 63, 81
Bounds, E. M. 33, 46, 59, 89, 155
Brainerd, David 156
Bramwell, William 91, 156
Brother Lawrence (Nicholas Herman) 147, 151
Bushnell, Horace 119
Cairns, Earl 156
Camus, Albert 163
Carmichael, Amy 13, 22, 23, 25
Chadwick, Samuel 13, 81, 83, 91–95, 110–12, 131, 142, 144
Chaim Weitzmann 148
Chambers, Oswald 133
Chapple, Stanley 34
Children 32, 33, 68, 69, 84, 85, 88, 98, 116–25, 135, 136. See also Family.
Church 10–12, 17, 19, 31, 32, 34, 44–48, 50–52, 55, 56, 60–64, 69, 74–78, 87–91, 127–31, 140–42, 157–63
Clark, Glenn 132
Clement of Alexandria 40
Coleridge, Samuel Taylor 72
College 64–65, 123, 124; conferences 57; spiritual awakening at 130
Commitment 22, 57–59, 66, 77
Communication 12, 33, 50, 72, 86, 124
Communion 9, 12, 19, 61, 82, 84, 86, 94, 153, 156
Communism 11, 55
Confession 38, 41, 43, 45
Conversion 74, 129, 146, 164. See also Salvation; Witnessing.
Conviction 90, 144
Crime 51
Cryderman, Dale 144
Cunningham, Glen 107
Davison, Leslie 78, 153, 154, 162, 167
Death and bereavement 24, 25, 30–32, 56, 83, 87, 139, 140, 162, 164, 166
Dedication 35, 38, 55, 146
DeRenty, Monsieur 156
Devotions, private 17, 31, 35, 86, 123, 138, 147. See also Solitude; Worship.
Dickens, Charles 114
Diet 106, 107. See also Healing.
Discipline 17, 21, 25, 28, 57, 90, 107, 110

169

Divine healing. *See* Healing.
Divorce 50, 51
Doctrine 86, 88
Dunning, Norman 144
Eckhart, Meister (Master) 166
Evangelism 47, 58, 77, 128, 159, 167. *See also* Salvation; Witnessing.
Faith 11, 12, 24, 30, 39, 51, 73, 80, 88, 90, 92–95, 97–100, 102, 111, 116, 124, 131, 137, 145, 149, 150, 155
Family 7, 10, 21, 31, 32, 41, 68, 69, 84, 96, 98, 116–18, 121–23. *See also* Prayer, family.
Fasting 47, 87, 140, 141, 162
Fellowship 34, 41, 46, 56, 71, 74, 75, 77, 113, 116, 118, 124
Fellowship of the Burning Heart 57, 59, 63
Fletcher, John 87, 155
Forgiveness 18, 24, 41, 101, 111
Forsyth, P. T. 153, 165
Francis of Assisi 87
Fraser, James 133, 156
Fulfillment 83, 151, 164, 165, 167; marital 117
Gesswein, Armin 46, 48
God 132–37; love of 27–28, 31, 32, 42, 85, 99, 135, 147–49, 144, 166; kingdom of 58, 65, 90, 91, 101, 108, 126, 127, 130; power of 11, 21, 39, 54, 58, 89, 97, 119, 138; righteousness of 49; will of 80, 83, 100, 110, 111, 137; witness of 127
Goode, Pearl 47, 48
Goodykoontz, H. G. 134
Gould, Al 58
Grace 16, 90
Graham, Billy 12, 47, 91, 143, 156
Graham, Ruth Bell 12, 91, 156
Great Awakening 63. *See also* Revival.

Guidance 10, 12, 35, 36, 38, 43, 66, 116, 128, 135, 141, 160
Halverson, Richard (Dick) 56, 57, 59, 63
Hatch, Edwin 31
Havelock, Henry 156
Haystack Prayer Meeting 63
Healing 7, 10, 81, 96–100, 101–3, 109–11, 131, 137, 139, 162; medical science and 98, 106, 111; mental health and 104; redemption and 109
Health 15, 16, 30, 32, 45, 101–4, 106–9, 111, 117, 140
Herbert, George 31
Helms, E. E. 103
Holiness 12, 35, 52, 82, 85, 163, 164, 167. *See also* Morals.
Holy Spirit 12, 16, 17, 25, 28, 30, 31, 45, 58, 62, 63, 71, 77, 82, 89, 94, 95, 141, 144, 146, 148–50, 163; as the Inner Voice 28, 36, 38, 71, 132, 146; Spirit-filled life 12, 15, 18, 31, 144
Home. *See* Family.
Hospital visitation 162–63
Humility 35, 118, 135
Hyde, John ("Praying Hyde") 37–39, 43, 45, 87, 90, 91
Jesus Christ 25–27, 60–62, 79–81, 84–89, 109–11, 147, 148, 150, 151, 159, 160; as Mediator 81; power of 109, 110; Scriptures concerning 25
Jones, E. Stanley 17, 23, 25, 29, 33, 72, 98, 99, 105, 112, 113, 117, 125, 135, 142, 149, 151, 153, 154, 166, 167
Judson, Adoniram 156
Juvenile delinquency 51
Kagawa. *See* Toyohiko Kagawa.
Keble, John 42
Kelly, Thomas 61, 78
Ken, Thomas 31, 155
Kingdom of God. *See* God, kingdom of.

Kunkel, Fritz 165
Lambert, D. W. 144
Leighton, Robert 155
LeSourd, Catherine Marshall 20, 112
Lewis, C. S. 49, 149
Leadership 128-29, 152ff., 160-62, 166, 167; pastoral 127; of prayer group 67, 78
Love 31, 40, 54, 62, 75, 130, 153, 164, 166, 167; marital 51, 115, 116; parental 120ff. *See also* God, love of.
Luther, Martin 155
McCheyne, Robert Murray 155
MacDonald, George 154
McLaughlin, Blaine E. 103
Marriage 21, 29, 32, 49-51, 113-19, 117, 119, 121, 125; husband 21, 32, 113-19; wife 13, 21, 29, 32, 33, 37, 51, 113-18, 128, 140, 155, 167
Martyn, Henry 155
Mears, Henrietta 56, 63
Menninger, Karl 101, 102, 111
Mental suggestion 103, 105, 111. *See also* Healing.
Mercy 12, 35, 91, 97, 99
Methodism 17, 70, 127; class meetings 70. *See also* Wesley.
Miracle 33, 48, 54, 91, 98
Missions 75
Mitchell, Hubert 69
Morals 49, 50
Mozart, Wolfgang A. 34, 41
Müller, George 22, 89, 156
Music 22, 32, 34, 154, 164
Nature 27, 34, 123; human 35, 53, 102, 126
Oda, K. 58
Parents 33, 51, 52, 109, 113, 119-21, 124, 129, 137. *See also* Children; Family.
Pastors 29, 38, 46, 47, 48, 49, 51, 52, 56, 57, 59, 64, 74, 75, 97, 127, 128, 139, 144, 157, 158, 160, 161
Pastors 46, 48, 64
Patience 39, 138
Payson, Edward 155
Peace 21, 23, 55, 56, 97, 134
Pentecost 17, 44, 62, 63, 82, 89, 116, 150. *See also* Holy Spirit.
Petersham, Maud and Mishka 68
Pierson, A. T. 44, 63
Power, spiritual 90, 101-3, 128, 130, 135, 144
Praise 29-32, 37, 41, 43, 72, 86, 105, 116, 122, 129, 155
Prayer, conversational 69, 70; daily 15, 19, 21, 25, 35, 45, 130; ejaculatory 39; family 68, 69, 113; group 15, 19, 63-65; 72, 147, 157, 160, 161; intercessory 39, 126, 140, 157; private 19, 38, 76; verbal 72, 114, 162
Prayer cell 11, 13, 44, 51, 60, 64-66, 71, 73-75, 78, 160
Prayer list 18, 28, 29, 39
Prayer meeting 45, 57, 63, 144
Prayer partner 19, 66, 124
Preaching 13, 22, 47, 52, 54, 81, 90, 107, 144, 145, 159
Pride 79, 86, 128, 141, 144, 145
Prison 52, 105
Quakers (Society of Friends) 74, 147, 148
Resurrection, last 111
Revival 7, 10, 11, 13, 19, 44-56, 59, 63, 65, 73, 77, 127, 129, 130, 144, 160; Evangelical 63; Korean 45; Moravian 45, 59, 127; Welsh 46, 48, 77
Righteousness 93, 123. *See also* God, righteousness of.
Rinker, Rosalind 69, 70, 78
Roberts, Evan 77
Robinson, Forbes 153
Russell, Merv 145
Rutherford, Samuel 155

Sacrifice 28, 55, 58
Salvation 33, 37, 41, 44, 57, 81, 88, 98, 101, 124, 130. *See also* Evangelism; Witnessing.
Sangster, W. E. 11, 13, 17, 20, 25, 29, 33, 34, 37, 38, 40, 43, 44, 48–55, 59, 64, 66, 76–78, 144, 153, 154, 157, 159–61, 167
Satan 22, 82, 109, 110
Scripture. *See* Bible.
Self 19, 29, 38, 41, 51, 54, 55, 57, 61, 62, 73, 75, 89, 103, 107, 116, 123, 148, 149
Sermon on the Mount 25, 36
Shedd, Charles W. 157, 162, 167
Sheppard, Dick 153
Silence 72, 156. *See also* Solitude.
Simeon, Charles 155
Slosser, Mary 22
Solitude 27, 31, 86, 130, 156. *See also* Devotions, private; Silence.
Spirit. *See* Holy Spirit.
Spiritual awakening. *See* Revival.
Spurgeon, Charles H. 46
Stanger, Frank Bateman 10, 96, 97, 100, 101
Sternberg, Brian 5, 166
Stewart, James S. 143, 144, 154, 155
Stowe, Harriet Beecher 27
Suffering 31, 53, 56, 81, 96, 97, 99, 103, 116, 133, 134, 137, 142, 160, 164–67. *See also* Healing.
Taylor, J. Hudson 91
Temptation 18, 32, 65, 66, 114, 118, 131, 141
Ten Commandments 24, 36, 49
Tennyson, Alfred 89
Thanksgiving 30, 34, 38, 43, 126, 141, 147, 159, 160
Theology 42, 61
Theresa of Avila 161
Thomas à Kempis 147, 151
Torrey, Reuben A. 94
Toyohiko Kagawa 22, 108
Turnbull, Ralph G. 143, 144
Tweedie, Donald Jr. 134, 138, 142
Van Valin, Clyde 97
Welch, John 155
Wesley, Charles 31, 147, 151
Wesley, John 17, 29, 35, 58, 60, 63, 65, 70, 87, 90, 106, 107, 143; devotional life of 29, 155
Weitzmann. *See* Chaim Weitzmann.
Whitefield, George 63
Will, human 80. *See also* Nature, human.
Witnessing 58, 75, 145, 146. *See also* Evangelism; Salvation.
Wordsworth, William 72
Worship 16, 34, 55; family 32, 113, 116ff.; and revival 45
Wyon, Olive 133, 142, 163, 164, 167

www.ingramcontent.com/pod-product-compliance
Lightning Source LLC
Chambersburg PA
CBHW050816160426
43192CB00010B/1784